The Employer Brand

The Employer Brand

Keeping Faith with the Deal

HELEN ROSETHORN,
MEMBERS OF BERNARD HODES GROUP
and
CONTRIBUTORS

GOWER

Published by
Gower Publishing Limited
Wey Court East
Union Road
Farnham
Surrey, GU9 7PT
England

Ashgate Publishing Company
Suite 420
101 Cherry Street
Burlington,
VT 05401-4405
USA

www.gowerpublishing.com

British Library Cataloguing in Publication Data
The employer brand : keeping faith with the deal.
 1. Corporate image. 2. Corporate culture.
 I. Rosethorn, Helen.
 658.3'14-dc22

 ISBN: 978-0-566-08899-5

Library of Congress Cataloging-in-Publication Data
Rosethorn, Helen.
 The employer brand : keeping faith with the deal / by Helen Rosethorn, members of Bernard Hodes Group and contributors.
    p. cm.
 Includes bibliographical references and index.
 ISBN 978-0-566-08899-5
 1. Employee retention. 2. Human capital--Management. 3. Corporate culture.
 4. Organizational behavior. 5. Personnel management. I. Bernard Hodes Group. II. Title.
 HF5549.5.R58R67 2009
 658.3'14--dc22

                                                              2009005472

Mixed Sources
Product group from well-managed
forests and other controlled sources
www.fsc.org Cert no. SA-COC-1565
© 1996 Forest Stewardship Council
FSC

Printed and bound in Great Britain by
MPG Books Ltd, Bodmin, Cornwall.

Contents

List of Figures   *vii*
List of Tables   *ix*
Acknowledgements   *xi*
About the Author   *xiii*
About the Contributors   *xv*
Foreword   *xxiii*
Preface   *xxvii*

PART I   **THE DEVELOPMENT OF THE DEAL**   1

Chapter 1   **Origins – Two Roots to the Family Tree**   3
                Helen Rosethorn
Chapter 2   **Methodology – A Concept in Action**   17
                Helen Rosethorn
Chapter 3   **Engagement – The Power of People**   35
                Annette Frem
Chapter 4   **Globalisation – Considerations for the Journey**   57
                Annette Frem and Helen Rosethorn

PART II   **THE DEAL IN PRACTICE**   71

Chapter 5   **Sense and Simplicity – Uniting the Employee and
                Customer Proposition**   73
                Jo Pieters and Job Mensink
Chapter 6   **From Poor M&S to Your M&S – The Historical
                Perspective**   89
                Keith Cameron
Chapter 7   **Learning the Lessons of History – All Over Again**   103
                Lou Manzi
Chapter 8   **Solving a Crisis Out of a Drama – The Passion Behind
                Social Responsibility**   121
                Sally Jacobson

Chapter 9   What's the Deal? The Impact of Legislation and New
                  Technology   137
               David Russell

PART III   STRIKING THE RIGHT DEAL   149

Chapter 10   Who Owns the Employer Brand? Asking the Question   151
               Helen Rosethorn
Chapter 11   From Business Case to Payback – The Challenge of
                  Meaningful Metrics   167
               Paul Crowsley
Chapter 12   The Future – Where Next for Employer Brands?   193
               Helen Rosethorn

Index   *213*

List of Figures

Figure 1.1   The brand and its stakeholders   5
Figure 2.1   The employer brand in action   20
Figure 2.2   Recognising that people are different at Tesco   22
Figure 2.3   Key stages on the employer brand journey   26
Figure 3.1   Key components of employee engagement   40
Figure 3.2   The brand balance model   42
Figure 3.3   House of Brands model   48
Figure 3.4   Branded House model   48
Figure 4.1   Expectations of employer branding   63
Figure 5.1   Touchpoints: the moments of truth   75
Figure 5.2   The employee value proposition house   77
Figure 5.3   Four stages in the talent–company relationship   78
Figure 5.4   Improving our position   79
Figure 5.5   Old and new communications   81
Figure 5.6   Circles of love: linking employees to the customer proposition   84
Figure 5.7   The inside story: interactive video portraits   85
Figure 5.8   The 4-C recruitment marketing framework in action   87
Figure 6.1   The virtuous circle   98
Figure 7.1a   SmithKline Beecham recruitment advertising campaign (1)   115
Figure 7.1b   SmithKline Beecham recruitment advertising campaign (2)   116
Figure 7.1c   SmithKline Beecham recruitment advertising campaign (3)   117
Figure 7.2a   GlaxoSmithKline recruitment advertising campaign (1)   118
Figure 7.2b   GlaxoSmithKline recruitment advertising campaign (2)   119
Figure 7.2c   GlaxoSmithKline recruitment advertising campaign (3)   120
Figure 9.1   The business goal   143
Figure 11.1   The measurement cycle   170
Figure 11.2   Measuring employer brand impact   173
Figure 11.3   Current versus desired employer brand image   178
Figure 11.4   Key components of employee engagement   179
Figure 11.5   The brand balance model   180
Figure 12.1   The most important CSR issue   195
Figure 12.2   Values, moral principles and ethics   197
Figure 12.3   Nike and the Personal Trainer   202

Figure 12.4   America's Army Online Recruitment Game   204
Figure 12.5   HBOS employee blog site   205
Figure 12.6   *Wall Street Journal* online careers fair   206

List of Tables

Table 2.1   Potential information sources for existing insight   29
Table 5.1   'Brand rituals' inspire employees to serve their customers
             better   85
Table 11.1   Feedback survey: summary of results, 2007   191

Acknowledgements

Selfishly, I would like to start by thanking a small core of Hodes people who made this happen.

Paul Crowsley, Annette Frem and Andy Rigden have all given of their precious home time to create their parts of this book and to help to weave the entire argument together. Thanks also to Andy Hyatt for his contribution to the final chapter. Luisa Calcinotto, in her role as our marketing manager, has also shown huge resilience for the task! And mention must be made of our production team who helped with the typesetting of the initial manuscript and all those models and diagrams.

Our contributors have equally been generous of their time and patient with the protracted process of getting to publication. Our thanks to:

Alex Batchelor – Royal Mail
Pam Bland – Ministry of Justice
Lee Broughton – Enterprise Rent-A-Car
Keith Cameron – Marks and Spencer
Laura Dolby – Bernard Hodes Group
Sally Jacobson – London & Quadrant
Elaine MacFarlane – GSK
Candice Maclachlan – Ministry of Justice
Lou Manzi – GSK
Job Mensink – Philips
Donna Miller – Enterprise Rent-A-Car
Juan Pemberton – Marks and Spencer
Jo Pieters – Philips
David Richardson – InnerVision
David Russell – William Hill
Jenny Strevens – Royal Bank of Scotland

Lorraine Taylor – Royal Bank of Scotland
Tony Freeman – Illustrator

And, finally, our thanks to Jonathan Norman at Gower Publishing who first mooted the idea of the book. He has stuck with us through thick and thin, and we appreciate his faith in our ability to pull it altogether.

About the Author

Helen Rosethorn, CEO, Bernard Hodes Group

A pioneer of employer branding practice in the UK, Helen Rosethorn is CEO of the Bernard Hodes Group. After successfully integrating the group into the Omnicom network a decade ago, she has built it into one of the UK's leading employment marketing and talent specialists.

An MBA at Bradford Management School crystallised Helen's long-standing interest in the people dimension and cultural dynamics of organisational success. It was here that Hodes's distinctive approach to employer branding had its origins. Developed and refined during more than ten years' practice with blue-chip clients, including GSK, Philips and Nokia, the Hodes's model examines the unwritten deal between employers and employees.

A member of Hodes's Global Network Executive Board, Helen is also a principal HR/Brand Strategy Consultant on talent, branding, engagement and communications projects. She speaks and writes widely about all these issues.

It is her great hope that the next few years will see more people at CEO level actively engage in the employer brand debate.

About the Contributors

Annette Frem, Bernard Hodes Group

Over the last 15 years Annette has specialised in HR, internal communications, sales and branding; most recently as International Culture and Leadership Manager within the France Telecom/Orange group.

Leading the Solutions practice, Annette is passionate about helping organisations identify their employer brand and engaging employees with their business culture and strategy. What's more, she believes they should have fun doing it! The key, she believes, is aligning the touchpoints of the employee lifecycle to ensure the development, reward and recognition of behaviour that demonstrates a company's internal and external brand and values. This is where companies can set themselves apart to attract and retain talent – and drive shareholder value.

Annette is a frequent speaker at European employer brand and employee engagement conferences.

Paul Crowsley, Bernard Hodes Group

With over ten years' experience in corporate insight and local area labour market analysis, Paul has a long-standing relationship with the Bernard Hodes Group. Currently Head of Insight, he was our Research Manager from 1999–2002 and, more recently, an Associate Consultant within our Solutions Consulting team.

Paul has run a wide range of research projects for clients, from analysis of local recruitment market conditions to major qualitative research programmes in the UK and overseas. His insights have underpinned the development of employer brands for Orange, GlaxoSmithKline, Tesco, HBOS and Laing O'Rourke amongst others.

Andy Rigden, Bernard Hodes Group

In a creative management and copywriting career that's mapped the rise of the employer brand, Andy has over a decade's experience of helping major organisations define and articulate their employer offers. He leads the proposition development and creative expression phase of our branding and engagement projects.

A graduate of Bristol University, Andy jointly leads the Bernard Hodes Group Creative and Production teams as Creative Director. He is an award-winning copywriter with extensive experience of expressing brands in the private, public and charity sectors.

Andy Hyatt, Bernard Hodes Group

Our Head of Digital, Andy has spent the past decade developing, evaluating and implementing operational and interactive marketing strategies for major blue-chip organisations across the globe. He has worked on both client and agency sides for some notable agencies and even more notable brands including Coca Cola, GSK, Mastercard, HP, Johnson & Johnson and Sky.

Heading up our team of developers and project managers and managing our third-party relationships, Andy drives the digital direction of Hodes. A frequent commentator on digital issues, he is the author of advisory papers on electronic and mobile commerce, as well as the use of digital media in advertising communications.

Alex Batchelor, Royal Mail (2005–2008)

Alex is the Executive Vice President – Marketing for TomTom, based in Amsterdam. Satellite navigation is a technology that is being adopted by customers faster than the mobile phone and the MP3 player, and TomTom is the clear market leader in Europe and growing fast in the US. Before his appointment at TomTom, Alex spent three years as Marketing Director at the Royal Mail, launching size-based pricing, managing a £250 million P&L and driving the introduction of tracking systems in mail sorting and with handheld devices. Alex has also worked for Orange (launching the brand in 20 countries), for Interbrand as the Managing Director and leader of the Brand Valuation practice, for Saatchi & Saatchi as a strategic planner and started his career at Unilever.

Pam Bland, Ministry of Justice

Pam joined the Ministry of Justice in February 2007 having previously led internal communications at Gloucestershire County Council. Prior to that, she was Head of Change Communications at the Home Office.

A graduate of University College London, Pam has worked at a senior level both in communications and HR, in the UK and New Zealand and within the public and private sectors. As Communications and HR Director for a large dairy company expansion she developed a successful, integrated communications approach across staff, shareholders and key stakeholders. She has since applied this approach to roles in the public and private sectors that have been supporting significant organisational and behavioural change.

Keith Cameron, Marks and Spencer (2004–2008)

After an introduction to industry via jobs in sales and production planning, Keith Cameron graduated from Bath University with a Social Science degree. He then held personnel management positions with Bestobell, Rank Xerox and Union Carbide before spending eight years as the Northern European Personnel Director of Levi Strauss. Two years were then spent as Personnel Director of Currys Ltd, following which he was appointed as Personnel Director of Storehouse PLC, covering the BhS, Richards, Habitat and Mothercare retail chains. He joined The Burton Group as Personnel Director of Debenhams in 1988, becoming Group Personnel Director in 1992 and was appointed to the Board in September 1994, having responsibility as an Executive Director for Operations, Logistics, Property, Shop Design & Development and Personnel. With the demerger of Debenhams in January 1998, he became Executive Director – Stores, Personnel & Operations for the restructured Group which began trading as Arcadia Group on 26 January 1998.

He has also been a member of the British Retail Consortium's Board of Management, Chairman of the Home Office's Retail Crime Steering Group and has served on the Executive Board of Industry in Education Limited.

Keith retired in 2001 but then returned to join Marks and Spencer in 2004 as HR Director. He retired again in 2008 and now has several non-executive directorships, including Barclay Bank Pension Fund, Britannia Building Society, Work Group plc and TacT Ltd.

Sally Jacobson, London & Quadrant Group (1987–2008)

Sally oversees approximately 1000 staff and is responsible for HR, training, facilities management, TUPE transfers and customer care. Under Sally's management, London & Quadrant has received the following prestigious awards: Investors in People, Charter Mark and Age Positive Champion. For the last five years the group has also been placed in the prestigious *Sunday Times* Top 100 Best Companies to Work for. Tower Homes, part of the L&Q Group, was placed at No. 1 on the *Sunday Times* Top 100 small/medium companies list in 2006, and won a special award for work–life balance. London & Quadrant has also been listed in the *Financial Times* 50 Best Workplaces in the UK for the last four years.

Sally's professional background began in the NHS starting as a student nurse in 1970 in Nottingham and progressing to Senior Nurse Manager at the Maudsley Hospital prior to joining London & Quadrant.

Elaine MacFarlane, GlaxoSmithKline

Elaine has worked in healthcare communications for more than 25 years, the last 11 of which have been spent at GlaxoSmithKline. Her team is responsible for corporate and global internal communications for GSK, corporate publications and design (including GSK's corporate identity), and the external website, gsk.com.

During the GlaxoWellcome/SmithKline Beecham merger, Elaine was a member of the merger integration team, coordinating merger communications across the two companies. She had previously been responsible for internal and external communications for the European Consumer Healthcare business.

Before joining SmithKline Beecham in 1997, Elaine worked in healthcare communications agencies involved in advertising, medical education, PR, branding, change management and medical writing. This included two years as founder and Managing Director of a UK-based office for a US agency network, and running her own company.

Elaine has a BSc in Microbiology and Genetics and a postgraduate business management qualification.

Lou Manzi, GlaxoSmithKline

Lou Manzi is Vice President, GSK Talent Solutions and has responsibility for overseeing the strategy and delivery of the global talent sourcing and recruitment functions at GlaxoSmithKline. He originally joined SmithKline Beckman Consumer Products as Manager, Government and Public Affairs in 1985. Prior to his current position, he was responsible for managing the leadership and succession planning process at SmithKline Beecham. During his tenure he has authored a variety of articles on recruitment metrics and how measures can operationally improve the recruitment function. He has also chaired many presentations on customer care, recruitment efficiency and is known for his entrepreneurial and creative approach to talent acquisition.

Lou serves on a variety of Boards including: the US Army War College: the Best Practices Institute, Waltham, Massachusetts; the Executive Grapevine, an organization comprising professionals in talent management, London, England; and Robert Michael Communications, Voorhees, New Jersey. He is also a former trustee of the Wilkes University Board of Directors.

Lou received his BA from St Mary's Seminary College and has done graduate work in the Executive Masters Program at the University of Pennsylvania.

Job Mensink, Philips

Job is responsible for the worldwide marketing of Philips as an attractive employer for talented individuals. Before joining the global Human Resources Team he worked in a range of strategy, marketing and innovation roles for Philips consumer and B2B businesses. Achievements include the development of globally standardized ways of working for end-user-driven innovation. He studied Innovation Management at Delft University of Technology and Economics at the Erasmus University in Rotterdam and is a passionate marketing teacher and guest lecturer at various institutes and universities.

Donna Miller, Enterprise Rent-A-Car

Donna Miller oversees all aspects of people development for Enterprise in Europe, which includes more than 4,700 employees. In her 18 years with the company, she has been instrumental in the recruitment growth for Enterprise in the US, Canada and Europe, and now serves as one of the company's officers.

Like the majority of Enterprise's officers, Donna began her career at Enterprise in the company's Management Training programme. Within one year of her start with the company, Donna was leading the human resources and recruitment efforts for one of the Southern California regions.

In 1997 Donna was promoted to Group Human Resources Manager in the New York/New Jersey area. In 1999 she was promoted to Corporate Human Resources Manager at Enterprise's corporate headquarters in St Louis, Missouri, to provide support to operating groups in Canada. In 2002 she was promoted to the position of Assistant Vice President/HR Director of Enterprise's human resources operations in Europe.

Jo Pieters, Philips

Currently Vice President Job Grading in Philips Electronics based in Amsterdam, Jo Pieters originally joined Philips as Recruitment Manager in 1989. In 1998 he joined Corporate HRM where he held various positions. In 2000 he was appointed Vice President eHRM and from 2001 to 2003 he was responsible for management development worldwide, including designing and rolling out an executive coaching programme for senior managers. From 2003 to 2007 he was responsible for creating a global recruitment function and establishing a strong employer brand worldwide.

Prior to Philips, Jo worked as a consultant in the Dutch government and was involved in management assessment, career counselling and executive search. He also worked for the University of Amsterdam and the Catholic University of Nijmegen, lecturing in statistics, research methodology, statistical computing and mathematical psychology.

Jo holds an MSc in Mathematical Psychology and a PhD in Social Sciences from the Catholic University of Nijmegen, as well as a certificate in organization design from the University of Southern California.

David Russell, William Hill

David Russell has worked within human resources for 30 years in the leisure, service and manufacturing sectors. The common theme throughout his working life has been highly people-intensive businesses, in which customer service has been paramount and the management of labour costs are a significant factor to the delivery of bottom-line profits. He is an HR generalist, always striving to work closely with line management to deliver pragmatic business solutions.

After an initial period in hotels and contract catering, he spent nine years within Alpha Airports Group, latterly as Human Resources Director for the airline catering division. Following a period as Divisional HR Director for Courtaulds Textiles, David joined William Hill, as Group Human Resources Director, in March 2001, just prior to the successful launch of the business on the London Stock Exchange.

David was brought up in Edinburgh and educated at Strathclyde University, where he undertook a degree in Business Studies and a postgraduate diploma in Personnel Management. He is a fellow of the CIPD.

Jenny Strevens, Royal Bank of Scotland

Jenny Strevens is the Group Manager of Employer Branding at the RBS group. Having joined RBS on the HR graduate programme in 2001, Jenny has now spent over seven years with the Group in a variety of HR roles, latterly focusing on group roles in talent management, communications and engagement and now devising and progressing the employer brand strategy at Group and UK level. With a background in applied psychology, Jenny has recently completed an MSc in Occupational Psychology, specialising in the psychological contract.

Lorraine Taylor, Royal Bank of Scotland

Lorraine is Group Head of Employer Brand at The Royal Bank of Scotland Group. She is responsible not only for the creation and development of a distinct and compelling employer brand for over 170,000 people working in more than 50 countries, but also for ensuring that the employee experience delivers on that 'brand promise'.

Lorraine has spent all her career within RBS, working largely within the retail businesses, creating and leading the service strategy for all RBS and NatWest branches and leading large-scale change programmes, as well as managing front-line business teams.

She has an MSc, is a Chartered Banker (FCIBS) and is a Member of the Chartered Institute of Personnel and Development.

Foreword

Almost 80 years ago, Margaret Mead, the American anthropologist, wrote *Growing Up in New Guinea* (1930). She looked at bonding customs, words and idioms, behaviour patterns, ritual festivals, rites of passage, body markings, tattoos and piercings, all of which, as she explained, were intended to underline and emphasize membership of the tribe or community. Although not the first, *Growing Up in New Guinea* was, in its day, one of the most influential books about the creation and maintenance of internal loyalties, or what now we might call brand engagement.

There is nothing in *The Employer Brand* that would surprise Mead, except perhaps its title and some of its more arcane jargon.

So if the ideas explored in *The Employer Brand* are so well known to anthropologists, what about the claim its editor Helen Rosethorn makes that employer branding only emerged seriously a few years ago, that it was pioneered in business schools and that it is only now beginning to make a real impact in the branding world?

The answer to this little conundrum is that Helen is quite right; a real understanding of anthropology is largely new in the world of branding and that's because of the way modern branding began. Its origins were in packaged goods for the housewife. Putting it simply, brands were initially just articles – ordinary household products sold over the counters of small grocery shops to a housewife of little means or education with a family and home to look after.

The product – jam or soap or whatever – was elaborately packaged and heavily promoted. Packaged goods companies drew their inspiration for promotional activities from patent medicine manufacturers whose dubious distinction was to peddle their quack remedies through grotesque exaggeration. Coca Cola, for example, was originally described as 'a valuable brain tonic and cure for all nervous afflictions'.

And that's where the unique selling proposition (USP) – the initials so beloved by so many branding people – comes in. Take a commodity product, the same as any other in price and quality and make it seem different and desirable through words and pictures; in the 1950s, when this kind of practice was at its apogee, Omo the washing powder, for example, had 'adds brightness to whiteness' as its unique selling proposition.

Over the period from about 1880 to 1980 branding continued to develop in its own particular idiom, even though supermarkets emerged and shoppers got a lot richer, better educated and canny and it all became much more sophisticated, because there was so much more choice.

Then in the 1970s, 1980s and 1990s, the world of branding genuinely began to mutate as a result of a number of developments – a proliferation of existing media, entirely new media, new techniques in retailing and so on, and, above all, the emergence of the service brand.

There is a profound difference between a product brand and a service brand. Product brands, especially fast-moving consumer goods (FMCG) brands are about a single transaction, which may be endlessly repeated but, give or take a bit, is always the same. One bar of Kit Kat is the same as the last, and the next. Kit Kat doesn't answer back, doesn't get tired, isn't anxious and always tastes the same.

A service brand is entirely different. Dealing with service brands often involves a long drawn-out, fraught transaction involving a number of people. Just think of flying from London to, say, Budapest; the entire experience from the traveller's point of view is about how the various service people in the airline and elsewhere behave. It's a journey – in more ways than one. Service brands are about people. In order for the service brand to work well, staff must, as they say, live the brand. But the people who represent the organisation are just people, they lose their tempers, get tired and anxious, and sometimes have just had enough that day, so managing a service brand – which means managing the people who work inside the organisation – is much more complex than looking after a product brand like Kit Kat.

Traditionally, of course, almost all the effort, ingenuity and money spent on managing and marketing product brands was externally directed. With a service brand, however, everything is turned on its head. The brand has to be internally directed, so that the people who work in the organisation and represent it to the outside world can act with clarity, cohesion and in an immediately recognisable and predictable fashion.

All this involves a great deal of mutual support and reliance between people from different parts of an organisation who may be unknown to each other. In other words, it demands the creation and maintenance of mutual trust. It is all much more reminiscent of tribal behaviours, bonding and all that, than conventional product branding. Because it works, employer branding has spread from service-based organisations to all kinds of companies today. As this book points out, product and retail branding companies are also heavily engaged in employer branding.

There are, of course, some significant differences between employer branding in large corporations and traditional tribal behaviour. First, you are born into a tribe and usually you don't leave it until you die, but you are recruited into a corporation and you frequently leave it to go somewhere else. Second, unlike an organisation, the tribe is largely about itself and not the outside world; it is internally, rather than externally, focused.

But these two caveats aside, the similarities between internal corporate behaviour and tribal behaviour seem to me considerable. Putting it another way, a bit more of the Starbucks Coffee drinking rituals would do employer branding no harm, nor would some understanding and appreciation of the history of the organisation to which the employee belongs. In Chapter 4 there is reference to Orange and the evolution of its culture, but I remain shocked by how little the people who work for Orange know about how it started, how it grew to be successful, its various owners and so on. Orange people have a lot to be proud of, but nobody tells them anything about their tumultuous, exciting and still quite short history.

All this brings me to my next and final point: why don't the people involved with employer branding take a very close look at some non-commercial institutions whose lifeblood is bonding and loyalty to comrades and to the institution as a whole? The organisation which best understands all this, and has done for centuries, is, of course, the army. For the ultimate lesson in employer branding see the play *Black Watch*[1] – the magnificent portrayal of the soldiers of Fife.

Oh, and I nearly forgot to say, enjoy Helen's book – I did.

Wally Olins
Chairman, Saffron Brand Consultants, Goring-on-Thames

---

1   *Black Watch* has won four Olivier awards in 2009, including Best New Play.

Preface

Bernard Hodes Group in the UK was approached three years ago to write a book on employer branding, which begs an obvious question. Why has it taken us so long? Well, there are a number of reasons – some purely practical but some evolutionary, too. I initially envisaged that the book would be solely owned by our then Head of Consultancy. It took me some time to realise that this project was bigger than a single person within Bernard Hodes and that, in fact, many of the ideas and perspectives we have on the subject are shared ones. Indeed, I think one of the great strengths of our approach to the subject is that we offer a coherent philosophy without limiting ourselves to one person's point of view. Arguably, it is possible for one person to articulate and define the concept from an academic standpoint. But the intention with the book was always to offer practical, real-world-based guidance and that calls for the expertise and fresh perspectives offered by a more collegiate approach.

Our sister companies within Omnicom have used this collaborative technique very successfully on similar book projects. What's more, I sensed that the timing was right for such an approach. I felt that the concept with which we had been pioneers in bringing to the fore with many organisations, large and small, local and global, was in danger of becoming a passing fad – lots of people were jumping on the bandwagon, some talking it up, others talking it down, but far too many were undervaluing its power and potential. This meant that a more wide-ranging response to the challenges facing the concept was needed – a response that would call on many people's talents within Bernard Hodes.

Our work in the realm of employer branding has evolved, but one aspect has never changed. We judge success as putting in place the insight and foundations to a more enlightened appreciation of workplace behaviours and a new framework for human resource management. This is not meant to sound missionary, although sometimes that feeling is hard to avoid.

Having said this, we fully recognise that every employer brand programme needs a compelling business case and simply becoming more enlightened about talent is not enough. What's important is the organisational performance improvement delivered by being 'talent centric' and this is where the real debate on ROI should be – and increasingly is – focused.

Although a range of contributors demanded far more organisation, I did think that it might allow us to speed up the process of writing and publishing a book. I was naïve. Not because of any lack of enthusiasm and commitment on the part of our contributors whom I cannot thank enough for their hard work and patience, but because of the challenge for all of us of trying to do this in our 'spare time'.

There are many observations on the world of work captured in this book, and I hope and trust that all who read it will come away having gained a clearer perspective on the concept of the employer brand. I fear that whilst I admire many of the other books that have emerged on the topic of late, they overcomplicate the concept and underestimate the organisational behavioural agenda around it.

There are no formulas and no magic bullets. If you buy this concept, then you must accept that it is about the way you do things in your organisation and about how you might need to change and develop to attract and retain the talent that you need to succeed. It is not about a project; it is about a journey to a new organisational way of life.

PART I

THE DEVELOPMENT OF THE DEAL

1

Origins – Two Roots to the Family Tree

Helen Rosethorn
Bernard Hodes Group

Let's begin by explaining the thinking behind the title, *The Employer Brand: Keeping Faith with the Deal*. The intention from the outset has always been to avoid another academic explanation of the employer brand concept and to offer organisations working in this area something with a more practical application. The focus of the book is on the experiences and perspectives of organisations that have applied employer brand practices, rather than on academic definitions of the concept. Indeed, we hope that by featuring case studies and first-hand accounts from practitioners, other organisations will learn from these experiences and be prompted to share their own insights.

The real-world experiences of organisations that have begun an employer branding journey is the substance of the book, but it is important to first set the concept in an historical context. The notion of the employer brand is still a relatively young one, but it has its origins in distinct schools of thought. Armed with knowledge of these schools and where the concept began, we shall be in a better position to assess its strengths today.

Where Did the Concept Originate?

The idea of the employer brand emerged in the early 1990s, and a number of people laid claim to its creation. Rather than playing Solomon and sitting in judgement on these competing claims, we are going to use this first chapter to examine the origin of the concept and trace its development.

There are two roots to the family tree of the employer brand. The first lies in recruitment communications linked to the growth of the power of the corporate brand and the second in occupational psychology and, in particular, in the idea of the psychological contract. These two threads go back some way and, for many years, operated in parallel. But in the last decade – influenced by another key factor that we shall discuss later – they have combined to propel the concept of the employer brand into the limelight.

Advertising and the World of Work

Recruitment communications emerged as a specialism within the advertising industry in the 1960s. Recruitment messaging had, of course, existed before then, but the creation of specialist teams and then dedicated businesses to meet the desire of organisations to smarten up their 'sits vac' advertising really came to fruition from around 1958 onwards.

In the UK the catalyst was probably the growth of the search and selection industry. This sector had developed a critical mass and, by the early 1960s, executive recruitment firms were queuing up to place advertisements in the broadsheets of the time. The market was not particularly talent-constrained, but the column inches of the newspapers in those days did have limits so there was a sense of competition based on image and brand. In his book, *The Employer Brand*,[1] Simon Barrow speaks about his early years in the advertising industry and the realisation that, as the specialism of recruitment communications matured, this sector could learn a great deal from classical marketing principles.

In the academic world a parallel development was taking place, which was to prove equally significant. Brand management was becoming recognised as a legitimate discipline and, for the first time, the 'people dimensions' of an organisation's brand were being acknowledged and debated. Arguably, Bradford Management School was at the forefront of this breakthrough. At the time, the institution was divided between two schools of thought. Argument and discussion in the Business Strategy faculty was focused on a series of core strategy models which explained organisational behaviour and commercial success but left people out of the equation, relegating them to a footnote in operational logistics. Then, in the opposing camp, sat Philip Kotler and *The Principles of Marketing*[2] Recognising that

---

1　　Simon Barrow and Richard Moseley, *The Employer Brand*, Wiley, Chichester, 2005.
2　　Philip Kotler and Gary Armstrong, *The Principles of Marketing*, Prentice Hall, Upper Saddle River, NJ, 2005.

people are the biggest costs on the profit and loss account for many organisations and therefore that cultural and people-focused forces are powerful organisational drivers, Kotler encourages businesses to look at their people as consumers and to view the relationship between employer and employees – whether past, present or future – in terms of consuming a career or job.

It was a shift in perspective that opened up all sorts of questions and possibilities. If employees are consumers, how should employers create, define and package the product? What sales and marketing strategies should they adopt towards the job and how should product reputation be managed? Clearly, the new insight gave brand a central and defining role in commercial success.

The thought leadership underway at Bradford Management School was crystallised in 1994 with the creation of the UK's first chair in Brand Management. The first occupant of the new faculty was Professor Marc Uncles, an enlightened marketer who laid many of the academic foundations in this area. Happily, one of his early initiatives was a collaboration with Hodes that resulted in the model shown in Figure 1.1, which remains at the core of Hodes's thinking today.

Clearly, we do not see the words 'employer brand'. Rather, the model presents the employer brand as a subset of a central corporate brand, rather

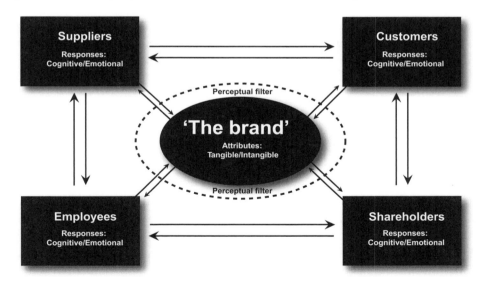

Figure 1.1   The brand and its stakeholders

than as a standalone element. The brand consists of the perceptions of a number of distinct, but connected, audiences, one of which is employees – past, present and future. The model also emphasises that for many organisations there is one 'master brand' and that – as covered later in this chapter and in this book – this overarching brand is gaining in importance and impact in organisational life.

In later chapters we will return to this model to assess its strengths and shortcomings, but it is worth highlighting its effectiveness at highlighting the relationship between the corporate and employer brand. It's clear the employer brand can't be defined, developed or managed in isolation from the corporate brand. Perhaps the relationship is not parent–child, but the two concepts are interconnected and we will examine exactly how once we have traced the development of the concept.

A World of Brands

At the same time as recruitment communications was coming of age the concept of the brand was gaining in momentum in many other ways. One of the best explanations of the journey of brands in recent decades has been written by the brand guru Wally Olins.[3] As he explains in *On Brand*, brands were once a simple assurance of basic quality and consistency for goods and services, whether they were everyday consumer products or a safe place to put your money. The first mass-market brands were patent medicines which flourished by making extravagant claims about the benefits they could bring to their consumers. In particular, they made their mark in the US where patent and proprietary medicines were huge business in post-Civil War America.

Led by household product companies such as Unilever and automobile manufacturers such as Ford, brands began to change, thanks largely to an explosion in consumer advertising. In the wake of this, brand owners and managers introduced a more rigorously scientific approach into their work, and a raft of advertising theories had developed by the 1920s. Perhaps the most high-profile of these was the notion of the USP – unique selling proposition – the characteristic that makes any product or service distinctive and therefore uniquely attractive. Interestingly, Olins pours scorn on this approach: 'Curiously, even today, among the more credulous and naïve members of the marketing fraternity, the initials USP still apparently possess some kind of credibility.'[4]

---

3   Wally Olins, *On Brand*, Thames and Hudson, London, 2003.
4   Ibid., p. 58.

Olins talks about the 1970s as being a turning-point in branding for five main reasons:

1.   the shift in power from manufacturer to retailer;

2.   the rise of new forms of promotion away from traditional advertising;

3.   new distribution systems and new media channels;

4.   the emergence of new brands like Nike, Body Shop and Benetton that were not just brands, but new concepts in themselves;

5.   an environment of wealth that was changing social, commercial and cultural behaviours.

We'd like to emphasise the fourth of these drivers because these organisations saw a future for branding that others only caught up with relatively recently. The Body Shop, led by its forward-thinking founder Dame Anita Roddick, was a case in point. The business redefined its sector and became part of a new breed of brands – a category that Olins summed up beautifully: 'Most of them simply ignored the division between product and retail; they were products *and* they were retail. The brand wasn't *in* the shop; it *was* the shop. And the brand was also the staff in the shop.'[5]

Roddick understood people power in building the Body Shop brand. In her book, *Body and Soul*,[6] she spoke candidly about how employees were a vital dimension of her brand:[7] 'How do you ennoble the spirit when you are selling something as inconsequential as a cosmetic cream? You do it by creating a sense of holism, of spiritual development, of feeling connected to the workplace, the environment and relationships with one another. It's how to make Monday to Friday a sense of being alive rather than slow death.' Roddick and the people behind these new brands understood that brands were at least partly built from the inside – 'bonding as much as branding' to use Olins' words.[8]

---

5   Ibid., p. 67
6   Anita Roddick, *Body and Soul: Profits with Principle – The Amazing Success Story of Anita Roddick and The Body Shop*, Ebury Press, London, 1991.
7   Ibid., p. 22.
8   Olins, *On Brand*, p. 16.

In the late 1800s and early 1900s this 'bonding' was centred on loyalty to a paternalistic or even philanthropic organisation. In the UK, places like Bourneville in York and Saltaire in Yorkshire exemplified this paternalistic form of affiliation, with large businesses providing villages for their workers and attempting to create a corporate family. But, as in every conventional family, there was a shared understanding of place and position. The hierarchy was set and supported by a well-developed command–and-control structure, although this was not a one-way relationship as members received fair treatment and a job for life.

The majority of businesses today don't operate on these lines, and the consumers of jobs have changed, too. Job security is a thing of the past as companies grow and shrink, hire and fire. 'Job consumers' in turn have more choice and less affiliation to a single employer. They vote with their feet, more freely and happily than before, and loyalty to a corporate purpose is much harder to create and sustain. Research shows again and again that employees feel more loyalty to their colleagues than to the organisation, and these priorities are particularly prevalent in the attitudes of Generation Y as discussed in more detail later in this chapter.

Branding has changed, and the focus is now on involvement and association, or 'the outward and visible demonstration of private and personal affiliation'.[9] Olin comments that 'when a brand gets the mix right it makes us, the people who buy it, feel that it adds something to our idea of ourselves'.[10] And, importantly, this is equally true of employees as it is of consumers. Today, this sense of affiliation to a corporate purpose is central to the people power of a brand and is at the heart of a strategic definition for employer branding.

Incorporating the Psychological Contract

Earlier, we referenced a second root to the family tree of the employer brand: occupational psychology.

Another iteration of the idea of 'bonding' to a corporate purpose is the more contemporary concept of 'engagement'. This notion has been at the top of the organisational agenda for some time, as it has a profound influence on corporate performance.

9   Ibid., p. 14.
10   Ibid., p. 16.

Since 1960, and particularly during the last 20 years, the examination of the psychological deal between employer and employee and its impact in the workplace has gained huge momentum. This has been reflected in the writings of Denise Rousseau and other academics. It's not clear who first coined the phrase 'the psychological contract', but Rousseau has certainly been a leader in exploring and developing the concept in recent times.[11] In the UK, Professor David Guest of King's College, London, and Mike Emmott from the CIPD have also done substantive work[12] using the CIPD's annual employee attitude survey to research the changing impact of the contract for both employers and employees.

According to Rousseau, the psychological contract is the foundation of employees' beliefs and behaviours in the workplace: 'From the recruitment stage of an employee's work life to retirement or resignation, it can have a profound effect on the attitudes and well-being of an individual.' And she continues: 'it is commonly understood as an individual's belief about the terms and conditions of a reciprocal agreement with an employer or manager; a belief that some form of promise has been made and that the terms are accepted by all involved'.[13]

The issue, of course, is that this is unwritten and, unlike the written employment contract the majority of us are familiar with, highly flexible, not necessarily clearly defined and extremely open to interpretation by both parties. And as Rousseau sets out in her definition, it inevitably has a significant and determining impact on people's behaviour and their demonstration of engagement or otherwise.

So why has 'engagement' grown in importance and apparently overtaken the psychological contract concept? It seems that the HR community has embraced the notion of 'engagement' because of its link to driving that elusive discretionary additional effort from employees that results in improved productivity and organisational success. Too few commentators appear to credit the psychological contract concept with a similar goal. Rousseau has been clear in her definitions. She sees the contract as a 'deal', going beyond mutual loyalty

---

11 D.M. Rousseau (1995) *Psychological Contracts in Organisations: Understanding Written and Unwritten Agreements*, Sage, London, 1995.

12 Mike Emmott, *Managing the Psychological Contract: Getting Value from CIPD Employee Attitude Surveys*, Chartered Institute of Personnel and Development, Professional Policy Committee, London, March 2004.

13 S.L. Robinson. and D.M. Rousseau (1994), 'Violating the Psychological Contract: Not the Exception but the Norm', *Journal of Organisational Behaviour*, 15 (1994), pp. 245–259.

and well-being and driving 'increased productive behaviour' – and we share her appraisal that the two concepts are very much in synchronisation.

From this position there is a natural link to the emergence of employer branding as a concept. Emmott comments on the model of the psychological contract as a useful way of addressing issues around people management. He suggests that the model is all about the delivery of a 'deal' and that, as the softer side of people management has come to the fore, the model has gained real traction.

Of course, the prize for many practitioners is understanding the 'unwritten' dimension of the employer– employee bond – and this edges us very firmly towards the employer brand idea.

Conway and Briner[14] have undertaken an evaluation of the psychological contract as a concept and have concluded that organisations have not been that successful in their attempts to make it more explicit. They suggest that organisations need to make more effort to understand what employees expect from the world of work and stress how subtle the dynamic of the contract can be. There is a need to understand how it plays out in everyday working life and how the balance of what is 'unspoken' can change so easily. Indeed, Conway and Briner, categorise the collapse of the contract as 'violation' – a very emotive and personal label.

One benefit from adopting a psychological perspective on workplace behaviour is the focus on its unpredictability. All day long – whether at work or at home – we seek to make sense of what is going on around us. The world of work appears to have become less predictable, and the secure paternalistic days of the nineteenth century seem a world apart from today's unforgiving working environment. And in sense, of course, perception matches reality since it is employees' perceptions of employers that is shaping their behaviours. Clearly there is a need to understand how perceptions are reached and therefore being framed. Conway and Briner talk about the stories that circulate in organisations to explain what is going on in working life and they stress the need for managers to understand and influence those stories. Managerial behaviours and the story-telling aspects of employer branding are themes that we will return to.

---

14 Neil Conway and Rob B Briner *Understanding Psychological Contracts at Work: A Critical Evaluation of Theory and Research*, Oxford University Press, Oxford, 2005.

This is now a useful moment to refer back to Figure 1.1 and the brand model developed in conjunction with Professor Mark Uncles. The figure shows the perceptual filters which are, of course, critical to understanding any brand, but vital to defining the brand through the eyes of employees, past, present or future.

These two roots to employer branding are taking us closer to a definition. However, before we attempt that, we need to consider in a little more detail the economic and social environment in which questions of employee attraction and engagement are being asked.

Enter the 'War for Talent'

It was three McKinsey consultants who coined the phrase 'war for talent' in the mid-1990s. The phrase 'people are our most important asset' had become an important part of the corporate vernacular – it seemed to be a mandatory requirement in most annual reports – and the notion of a talent war seemed to reflect this focus on people. The phrase was rapidly widely adopted, although most commentators imagined it was a passing fashion – and, to some extent, when the dot.com bubble burst a few years later they were proved right. However, in recent years the 'war for talent' notion has regained currency, perhaps understandably given the underlying demographic challenges faced by the major Western economies. Consequently, many organisations now find themselves back on the battle lines.

It's fair to say that there has been a shift in meaning behind the 'war for talent'. Although the global demographic changes which originally underpinned the term remain unaltered, the phrase is now generally used in the context of attracting and retaining talent. Today, the 'war for talent' is more often used to describe an organisation's fight to attract and keep the right people, rather than to delineate the unprecedented global mismatch between talent supply and demand in the industrialised world and, increasingly, in the emerging economies, too.

From a supply point of view, talent, as we currently know it, is changing. The population is ageing. This trend is going to be most dramatic in Europe and Japan. By 2025 the number of people aged 15 to 64 is projected to fall by 7 per cent in Germany, by 9 per cent in Italy and by a staggering 14 per cent in Japan. Even in China there will be a squeeze as a result of its one-child policy.

At the same time life expectancy is growing. As the over-55 age group increases in many nations, they face a need to work longer in order to afford a later and potentially longer retirement.

These changes are not decades away – they are here now. In the US there is about to be a huge leadership drain with a consultancy recently predicting that the 500 largest US companies will lose half their senior managers in the next five years or so as the baby-boomers begin to retire. Add to this the latest predictions from the US Bureau of Labor Statistics suggesting that by 2010 the country will face a shortfall of 10 million in its workforce and an unemployment rate of just 2 per cent, and it is clear that in many countries the demographic time bomb is about to explode.

While this time bomb has been ticking, there has been another socioeconomic shift of huge relevance to employer branding. The industrialised nations have moved from being producing economies to service economies, and, as a result, the value of companies has become far less about hard assets and much more about intellectual ones. In 2007 *The Economist* reported that intangible assets have shot up from representing 20 per cent of the value of companies in the S&P 500 index in 1980 to around 70 per cent today. We only need to look at the reach and influence of companies like Google, Goldman Sachs and Microsoft to realise that their strength lies in their intellectual capital – their people. As a result, there are those who eloquently argue that a CEO's primary responsibility has changed from the access and management of capital to the access and management of talent.[15]

As the attraction and retention of talent has turned into make-or-break factor for organisational success, HR professionals have had to develop a more detailed appreciation of the global talent landscape. Talent has always deserved to be a strategic issue, but now it is certainly hitting many more top-table agendas. Organisations are being forced to consider their options like never before – from where the right talent pools exist and moving business operations to take advantage of them, to looking at what it takes to move the talent to meet the business need. For some, outsourcing has worked; for others, it has produced mixed results. The geographical point of engagement is relevant, and we will discuss this in Chapter 4. But in the meantime let's take a closer look at the issue of the employee's shifting mindset and, in particular, at new entrants into the workforce.

---

15   Michael Gregoire, President and CEO of Taleo Corporation, 'The New War for Talent', ZDNet, 28 November 2007 at: http://news.zdnet.com/2100-9595_22-177886.html.

High-maintenance Employee Behaviours

The talent segment which has attracted the most attention of late has been Generation Y. There are various definitions about who constitutes Generation Y, but, for our purposes, we are assuming that it comprises people born between 1977 and 1995. Clearly, not everyone in this group has entered the workforce yet, but the vast majority has. And during their time in work they have shown that they are very different from previous generations – with very distinctive views about how, if at all, they will offer up their loyalty to employers.

Provocatively, a 2007 article in *Fortune Magazine*, entitled 'You Raised Them, Now Manage Them' neatly captures the challenge organisations are facing in engaging Generation Y:

> *This is the most high-maintenance workforce in the history of the world. The good news is that they are also going to be the most high-performing workforce in the history of the world. They walk in with more information in their heads, more information at their fingertips – and, sure, they have high expectations, but they have the highest expectations first and foremost for themselves.*[16]

Why is this? It sounds deceptively simple, but, as parents will testify, children are the output of the environment they are brought up in, and the upbringing of this generation, has, for many, been very different to those of their parents. Every parent classically wants more for their children, but Generation Y have been offered 'step change' when it comes to opportunity. Many members of Generation Y, however, have seen their parents make substantial sacrifices to create such opportunity and have decided that these don't merit the resultant rewards. Long working hours, work-induced stress, job insecurity and a family life governed by the financial necessity of dual breadwinners combine to create an unappetising prospect for many in Generation Y – and one that they have seen at first hand in their parents' generation. They don't like the look of 'struggle and sacrifice', so they have some strong views about what life needs to be like and how employers should behave.

In the *Fortune* article an audit associate at KPMG comments on his relationship with the firm and how they offered him flexibility around

---

16 Nadira A. Hira, 'You Raised Them, Now Manage Them', *Fortune Magazine*, 28 May 2007, pp. 38–46 at p. 28. This quote is attributed to Bruce Taglan, founder of operational research firm RainmakerThinking.

pursuing his out-of-work passion: 'It made me say, "You know what? This firm has shown a commitment to me. Let me in turn show some commitment to the firm". So this is a merger, if you will – between me and KPMG.'[17]

There is a great deal to learn from this particular quote. Generation Y need to feel, first, that the deal comes from the employer and, second, that it is a meeting of equals, and they are not subordinated, when it comes to that deal. But this commitment is fragile, it seems. One of the characteristics that marks this generation out most clearly is their willingness to vote with their feet when they become dissatisfied with an employer and leave their job without another one to go to – a trait that surely reflects both their high expectations of work and the security and opportunity they have to return home to their parents.

So, when it comes to loyalty, the companies they work for are down the list behind family, friends and colleagues. When they feel loyalty at work, it is a result of a connection with their colleagues and their immediate boss[18] – they want a sense that their immediate circle of influence values their contribution, shares their values and protects them from the work pressures that their parents experienced. Equally, they need to know where they are going and how their employer is going to help them get there.

These new rules of employee engagement are clearly critical to the question of understanding employer brands.

Brand Transparency

There is one more very important point to be made about brands before drawing the threads of this discussion together. It is directly linked to an appreciation of the behaviours of Generation Y, although it is by no means exclusive to that group.

We have talked about the unwritten aspects of an employer–employee deal and the impact of managerial behaviours and stories in the workplace on shaping perceptions. We have explored the beliefs of the new generation entering the workplace, with their ideas shaped by their observation of parental

---

17 Ibid., p. 28.
18 Jason Ryan Dorsey,*My Reality Check Bounced! The Twenty-something's Guide to Cashing in on Your Real-World Dreams*, Broadway Books, New York, 2007.

experiences. But that's not the whole story. We referred earlier to the emergence of brands as 'sense makers' for the consumer and the employee. If they are providing order to the chaotic world we live in, where else are we getting the evidence from to make this assessment?

Returning to Figure 1.1, we see that we look at any brand from a number of directions. It is also important to remember that, as individuals, we can find ourselves in all those boxes in the way we 'consume' brands. For example, I could be an employee of Tesco, own shares in Tesco, shop at Tesco and have a family member who is a supplier to Tesco. As a result, I would have a great deal of experience to put in my mental filing cabinet marked 'Tesco' from which to shape my views of that organisation. And, importantly, I don't just stock that filing cabinet with the items that Tesco provide.

Brand audiences have never been as discerning and as connected as they are today. Their access to information that will potentially shape their views has exploded, and this wealth of experiences and data shouldn't be underestimated. But the information revolution isn't a passive, one-way affair. For Generation Y – and other generations, too – the Internet isn't just a repository of knowledge, but also an opportunity to share one's own hopes, fears, preferences and passions. The digital transformation that has become known as Web 2.0 means that the Internet is no longer the gigantic library many thought it once was. Now it is the largest collection of communities the world has ever seen – an unrivalled forum for knowledge-sharing, business-bashing and score-settling, and the leisure activity of choice for millions of people around the world.

Employer reputations are being discussed, shaped and shared in a way that organisations can no longer regulate as they have done in the past. This new digital world and the information revolution means that their reputations are riding out in cyberspace partly out of their control, at the mercy of social networking and judged by audiences who can make their voices heard like never before. We believe what someone tells us on Facebook about what it is like to work for a certain company rather than what we read on a careers site. The 'truth' is what we hear from someone we have probably never met but who we've just traded opinions with on a discussion thread in a chatroom we've just joined. It brings new meaning to the words 'brand transparency'. And it casts organisational story-telling in a whole new light and pushes the employer brand firmly on to the corporate reputation agenda.

Summarising the Evolution

In the UK, the roots of the concept of the employer brand lie in the recruitment communications industry of the 1980s and 1990s and in a changing interpretation of the contract between the employer and employee at the turn of the twenty-first century. The concept emerged at a time when brands in general were taking on a whole new meaning, providing a sense of order to the consumer and organisational glue to the employee. However, given the deregulated digital world in which we live, organisations are finding that trying to regulate brands and brand behaviours is tougher than ever before.

The psychological contract is a powerful aspect of understanding employer brands, reminding us that there are 'unwritten' parts to the deal that an organisation establishes with its people. Some of these unwritten elements are tangible but generally they are intangible, caught up in the experience of employment, often delivered by an immediate boss and also enshrined in organisational stories and myths.

The concept has accelerated to the top of the corporate agenda because of the issues of talent supply and demand. In the main, this is down to global demographics, but it is also linked to the emergence of new global industrial economies, as well as changing attitudes to the world of work held by the next generation entering the workplace.

In Chapter 2 we will look at employer brand definitions, distinguish between employer branding and employer brand management and examine the methodologies that have emerged to define and develop employer brands.

2

Methodology – A Concept in Action

Helen Rosethorn
Bernard Hodes Group

As yet we have not committed ourselves to an employer brand definition. In this chapter we will do exactly that and try to negotiate some of the confusing jargon which surrounds the concept.

We will also look at the methodology which we at Hodes have developed to help organisations define their employer brand and, more importantly, manage that brand in day-to-day organisational life.

Defining the Concept

The next few thousand words of this book could happily be absorbed into a long list of all the various definitions of the employer brand which have emerged in the last few years. That would be unproductive. Instead, we are going to focus on the views of some thought-leaders and examine the consistencies and differences between competing theories before presenting what we consider to be a more rounded and practical descriptor for the concept.

An early, but simple, definition came from Andrew Mayo, the much admired Professor of Human Capital Management, Middlesex University Business School:

> *It is what is communicated – consciously or unconsciously – to every employee or prospective employee.*[1]

---

1   Andrew Mayo, *The Human Value of the Enterprise*, Nicholas Brealey Publishing, London, 2001, p. 123.

A more frequently quoted explanation comes from Simon Barrow already referred to in Chapter 1. Simon was an early exponent of the concept – many credit him with its origination. He defines the employer brand as:

> ... the package of functional, economic and psychological benefits provided by employment and identified with the employing company. The main role of the employer brand is to provide a coherent framework for management to simplify and focus priorities, increasing productivity and improve recruitment, retention and commitment.[2]

More recently, Libby Sartain, Senior Vice President of People at Yahoo, and co-writer Mark Schuman offered their view:

> It frames how you motivate employees to deliver what your business promises to customers and how you nurture a working environment that prospective employees will want to join.[3]

Hodes's own former Head of Consulting, Tom Crawford, offered a controversial view in 2006:

> I believe your definition will roughly reflect the evolution of HR in your business. Where HR is not seen as a strategic partner vital to the commercial success of the organisation, you may well sell the Employer Brand as a concept but I'd bet it is potentially limited to being an exercise in recruitment advertising.[4]

The most up-to-date definition comes from the Chartered Institute of Personnel and Development and their 2006 guide to the topic:

> ... a set of attributes that make an organisation distinctive and attractive to those people who will feel an affinity with it and deliver their best performance within it.[5]

---

2   Simon Barrow and Richard Mosley, *The Employer Brand*, John Wiley & Sons, Chichester, 2005, p. xv.
3   Libby Sartain and Mark Schumann, *Brand from the Inside*, Jossey-Bass, San Francisco, 2006.
4   Tom Crawford, 'To Brand or Not to Brand', in B. Anand Rao and Payal Baid (eds), *Employer Branding, Concepts and Cases*, Icfai University Press, Panjagutta, 2006, p. 238.
5   Paul Walker, 'Employer Branding: A No-nonsense Aproach, http://www.cipid.co.uk/surveys.

There are some key similarities and some important differences emerging in these definitions. The similarities centre on attributes, distinctiveness and engagement of existing and future employees.

The notion of the brand as an array of elements is a consistent theme. What's more, many observers comment that the packaging of these elements creates a 'unique selling proposition' which in turn, needs to appeal to existing and potential employees. As Tom Crawford has noted, too often attention is purely focused on the attraction agenda and Andrew Mayo's early definition was interestingly framed solely in this setting.

Conversely, one of the most significant differences is that some commentators limit their definitions to discussions of 'attributes' and 'features'. They fail to translate these qualities into tangible and distinctive benefits identified with the employer and relevant and motivating to employees.

A further key – and worrying – difference is the line of sight to the organisational purpose and end-customer. The definitions do not clearly and consistently remind us that there is no point or sustainability to the employer brand if it does not serve the end-game of the organisation – and, of course, improve employee satisfaction.

It's often overlooked that every organisation has an employer brand, and an examination of this is a good starting-point for any practitioner interested in this concept. Just as every individual represents a certain kind of person offering a certain kind of relationship and delivering a certain kind of value in a network of friends and family, every organisation has an employer reputation. Few commentators spell this out, although this has been described as the 'default employer brand'.[6]

A Concept in Action

We promised a definition:

> *An employer brand is in essence the two-way deal between an*
> *organisation and its people – the reasons they choose to join and the*

---

6   David Lee, 'The True Power of a Magnetic Employer Brand in Employer Branding, Concepts and Cases', in B. Anand Rao and Payal Baid (eds), *Employer Branding, Concepts and Cases*, Icfai University Press, Panjagutta, 2006.

reasons they choose – and are permitted – to stay. The art of employer branding is to articulate this deal in a way this is distinctive, compelling and relevant to the individual, and to ensure that it is delivered throughout the lifecycle of the employee within that organisation.

Our view is that to really define and manage your employer brand it is best viewed as comprising two elements: These are a proposition – the validated definition of that deal – and an employee experience – the reality of the delivery of the deal (see Figure 2.1).

The Employee Value Proposition (EVP)

Marketers teach us the concept of creating value in the eyes of the consumer or customer. The product offers the consumer or customer the promise of the delivery of a certain set of attribute(s) and/or experience(s). The consumer or customer keeps on coming back if that promise is met and that product or service continues to meet their specific needs – because we have to remember that tastes and needs move on.

There is a lot of confusion between labels like employer brand proposition and the employee value proposition (EVP).

The EVP needs to be seen in the same light as the customer proposition. It offers us the opportunity to capture the impact or benefits of the 'written and unwritten' aspects of the psychological contract referred to in Chapter 1.

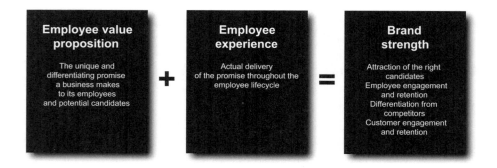

Figure 2.1   The employer brand in action

Some writers have produced complex models attempting to explain where the EVP fits in with the employer brand. The confusion often stems from the fact that there is 'one brand'. As we have noted earlier, there is no separate employer brand and, for the employee dimension to add strength to the 'one brand', it has to be linked to the overarching brand promise or proposition.

Some EVP definitions are only focused on the benefits to the employee. However, given the need for that employee to deliver value back to the organisation for the deal to be sustained, we prefer an EVP definition which captures the sense of fulfilment for both sides of the deal.

For many large and complex organisations, the drive to reach this overarching articulation sometimes feels like the search for the lowest common denominator rather than the highest common factor. The real measure of an effective EVP is its ability to translate into effective subpropositions for the audiences it serves – which we can describe as talent segments.

To return to the 'product' world for a moment, think about the power of the BMW brand and its promise of 'the ultimate driving machine' to its customers. Then consider how this is translated into the product promise to serve those who ride BMW motorbikes as well as those who dig deep into their pockets for their 7 series. These are very different product articulations with very different attributes – but linked by the 'golden thread' of engineering excellence.

GlaxoSmithKline, for instance, has summarised its EVP through the tag-line 'Together we can make lives better'. However, it recognises that how this plays out as a deal for the individual is different from how it plays out for the pharmacist producing compounds in the lab and the salesperson selling the company's latest vaccines to medical personnel.

Another vital aspect to appreciate in looking at segmentation in relation to employer brands is that whilst skills groups can offer one dimension of segmentation, there are other equally valid dimensions. Maslow's Hierarchy of Needs[7] offers one such alternative method of segmentation. A more up-to-date interpretation of this, based on extensive research with 24 US corporations, has been published by Tamara J. Erickson of the Concours Institute.[8] Her model suggests that work plays six general roles which correspond to six general types

---

7   A.H. Maslow, 'A Theory of Human Motivation', *Psychological Review* 50 (1943), pp. 370–396.
8   Tamara J. Erickson and Lynda Gratton, 'What It Means to Work Here', *Harvard Business Review*, 85 (March 2007), pp. 104–112.

of employee based on psycho-demographic characteristics. Each segment cares deeply about several aspects of the employee–employer relationship such as 'structure or routine' or 'stimulating tasks that enable continual leaving and growth', but little about others.

One organisation that has attracted substantial coverage about its use of segmentation to develop its employee proposition is Tesco. A key factor in Tesco's emergence as a world force in retailing has been its understanding of customer behaviours and, in particular, what drives customer loyalty. However, in 2000 CEO Terry Leahy was concerned that the organisation did not have the same level of insight into what drove the loyalty of their people. As a result, Tesco established a People Insight Unit under the direction of David Richardson, who launched research to identify the employer brand drivers for the organisation. Segmentation was fundamental to David's work – in the first instance, by cutting the data to identify groups by loyalty, role and attitude. The resultant attitudinal groupings yielded the insight that loyalty was at its highest at the two ends of the spectrum – for those who 'live to work' and those who 'work to live' – but that it played out in different ways in between (see Figure 2.2).

Interesting correlations emerged, such as the links between emotional loyalty and absence and between functional loyalty and attrition. Moreover, the

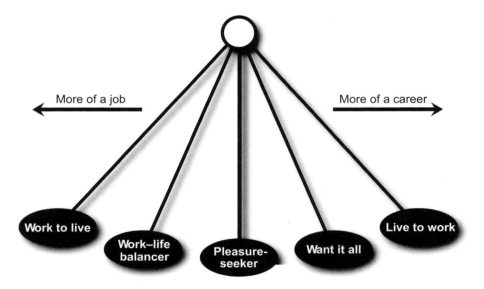

Figure 2.2   Recognising that people are different at Tesco

research helped Tesco recognise that people pass through different attitudinal groups during their working lives.

The impact of this segmented approach to research went far beyond mere diagnosis and a better understanding of the employee value proposition. Indeed, the organisation made changes to some of its working practices as a result – notably, improving its approach to flexible working.

The Employee Experience

It feels like a major disservice to tackle this in a few paragraphs, but other contributors will discuss this topic in more detail in future chapters. The vital point to make here is that the EVP is nothing more than a car in a showroom – we're sticking with our BMW analogy – without the 'road-testing' of the employee experience.

In Chapter 3 Annette Frem discusses the employee lifecycle, and in Chapter 5 Philips bring this to life through their touchpoint table. In Chapter 1 we also talked about the world of work in terms of delivering the reality of the psychological contract. Of course, we are in fact talking about perceptions, but the perceptions we form of the delivery of our deal with the organisation are the measures by which we are engaged or otherwise and deliver the performance required of us or not.

Because interest in the employer brand has, to date, been driven by the war for talent, too often the lifecycle focus has not been holistic. It has been too much about recruitment and not enough about life beyond on-boarding. However, a new debate about which parts of the lifecycle carry more weight than others is emerging. Again, this is nothing new to the marketers. They aim to hook and retain us as customers by dealing with any 'cognitive dissonance'[9] swiftly and effectively – the whole CRM discipline has grown up on the back of this. Disney has long talked about its 'magic moments' for visitors to its theme parks – points in the customer experience of particularly high impact and highly important to the brand proposition. Mickey Mouse's signature in the autograph book is one of the most well known.

---

9   A definition of cognitive dissonance would be: 'A state of psychological discomfort arising when a consumer tries to reconcile two conflicting states of mind, for example, the positive feeling of having chosen to buy a product and the negative feeling of being disappointed with it afterwards.'

If organisations really are to manage their employee experience as part of managing their employer brand, this is a key part of the lifecycle requirement. What are the pivotal points on the employee journey when the deal is sealed or otherwise? Of course, recruitment will feature in a big way, and today organisations like Google speak proudly of the power of its recruitment processes in selecting a future 'Googler'.

Lynda Grattan has written recently about 'hot spots'[10] as the hallmark of the most successful and progressive organisations. These are the times and places within businesses and teams where cooperation flourishes, creating great energy, innovation, productivity and excitement. Within her formula for 'hot spots' she points to the power of the 'signature experience' and defines this as 'a visible, distinctive element of an organisation's overall employee experience. In themselves, signature experiences create value for the firm but they also serve as a powerful and constant symbol of the organisation's culture and values.'[11] Google's recruitment process, for instance, is one of its signature experiences.

Other organisations like Starbucks talk about 'internal brand rituals' which bind their employees to the customer proposition and in turn offer value back to their people. The key brand ritual at Starbucks is their coffee tasting.

All this emphasises the point that the employee experience element of defining and managing an employer brand is not about 'one look or feel', starting with recruitment communications. It is about understanding the core deal, understanding how it plays out across the talent segments, understanding how it has to hit the right balance between aspiration and reality to attract and retain and then manage the organisational behaviours accordingly throughout the employee journey. This is not to say that employer brand communications do not have their place. There is a whole raft of employee and prospective employee communication tools with which to enshrine a message and tone of voice about the 'deal'. But the behaviours must be right first.

The Right People Doing the Right Things for the Right Reason

Before looking at a methodology for defining and managing the employer brand, there is one further important point to cover. In Chapter 1 we looked at

---

10   Lynda Gratton, *Hot Spots: Why Some Teams, Workplaces, and Organizations Buzz with Energy – and Others Don't*, FT Prentice Hall, London, 2007, p. 106.
11   Erickson and Gratton, 'What It Means to Work Here', *op. cit.*

the origins of employer branding and the organisational, social and economic factors which have supported its emergence as a powerful concept in the world of human capital management.

In the rush to respond to these pressures, and to some extent supported by the early recruitment communications-centric definitions of employer branding, companies have been urged to become 'best places to work' or 'employers of choice'. But it's legitimate to ask: are these real routes to organisational success?

Lynda Gratton's research,[12] referred to earlier, has revealed that companies that successfully create, live and communicate signature experiences understand that different types of people will excel at different companies and that all employees do not want the same thing. The high-performing organisations she studied were clear on the kind of people who worked well and would buy into their culture and working patterns. This is not to say that they were not prepared to adapt and be creative – and many developed signature experience responses to accommodate the people they identified as right for them. Similarly, research by Dr Brian Smith of the Cranfield School of Management[13] for *The Sunday Times* Employer Brand Conference in 2007 emphasised that exemplary employers understood that they could not synthesise an employment experience that was not rooted in their cultures.

So, we would like to hammer a final nail into the coffin of 'employer of choice'. Organisations should instead aspire to become the employer of choice for the 'employees of choice' – those individuals that they know are right for them and vice versa.

A Classical Methodology

There are a number of methodologies to help organisations define and manage their employer brands. There are also some excellent sources of insight and ideas, but, in our experience, practical 'how-to' guidance is still rare. It was this gap that led the UK's Chartered Institute of Personnel and Development to create something for its own members.[14]

---

12 Ibid.
13 *Values Based, Integrity Driven: How Leading Companies Create and Use Their Employer Brands*, June 2007.
14 Paul Walker, *Employer Branding: A No-Nonsense Approach*, CIPD, October 2007. Available at: http://www.wdad.co.uk/pages/pdfs/downloads/Employer%20Branding%20Guidelines.pdf.

In the rest of this chapter we will take you through the methodology we have established successfully within the Hodes consulting practice over the last eight years. It's worth emphasising two key points:

1.   Whilst it is a framework with five key stages, it is best seen as a journey. It takes time and it does not always follow the course that you initially designed.

2.   It is based on a classic strategic brand development framework – but it is not a one-off event. It is a really a continuum and, as such, metrics should inform a view on the effectiveness of the brand and the need to adjust its proposition and delivery.

The journey diagram depicted in Figure 2.3 shows five stages. These follow an hour-glass pattern, narrowing down from a wide gathering of vision and insight to define the 'proposition' and then widening out as that proposition is implemented and managed. There is both an internal and external dimension to all activity.

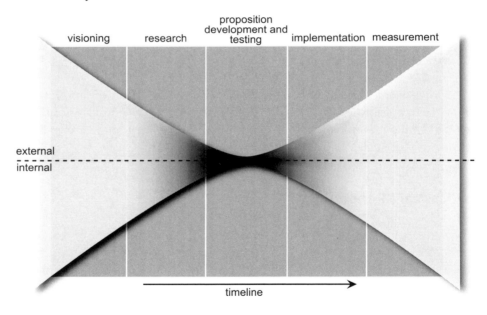

Figure 2.3   Key stages on the employer brand journey

STAGE 1: VISIONING

Core Activities	Core Outputs
Project scoping	Project plan and timeline
Objective setting	KPIs
Stakeholder mapping	Steering group
Stakeholder engagement	Project team
Project positioning and internal communications Needs analysis	Internal communications plan
Initial research design and talent segmentation	Outline research plan

This is the vital scoping and objective-setting phase (and, in our view, should come after the initial business case is established). It typically involves time spent answering a number of questions and establishing the lead stakeholder team and the wider stakeholder group (which could include partners external to the organisation if relevant) that any employer brand journey will need to involve along the way. Stakeholder involvement can be defined at a number of levels, but establishing the core ownership team at the outset is critical.

Chapter 10 looks at the question of who owns the employer brand and points to key stakeholders that must be engaged. We passionately believe this should be on the radar of the top man or woman, but we also recognise that getting them to participate in a steering group might be unrealistic. However, our suggested wish-list would include the lead representatives for the following areas:

- Senior team;

- Marketing (including any in-house brand design groups);

- HR;

- Internal Communications (if not covered within HR or Marketing);

- Corporate Communications (if not covered within Marketing);

- Special strategy groups.

It is also essential at this stage to define key talent groups and the geographical scope that will be involved to assess perceptions of the brand as an employer. Making the link to relevant customer segmentation is useful, but the driver must be the talent agenda – with talent defined in the widest sense and fundamentally linked to the organisational goals.

STAGE 2: RESEARCH

Core Activities	Core Outputs
Existing insight audit	Additional research requirements
Internal employee brand engagement research	Employer brand engagement analysis
External potential and past employee brand engagement research	
Competitor analysis	
Gap analysis	Brand-driver mapping
Touchpoint mapping	Touchpoint analysis

Research varies in scale and complexity for every organisation. Typically there would be two objectives to this stage – an understanding, of, first, how the organisation is perceived as an employer by defined talent groups within the organisation and, second, how the brand is perceived as an employer by the same defined talent groups outside the organisation – plus, of course, an analysis of the gap that may exist between the two.

Many organisations are sitting on existing data which can provide a head-start to this phase – large organizations, in particular, are classically 'data-rich, information-poor'. Some kind of internal insight audit is a valuable first step. The challenges of using existing insight are set out in Chapter 1, but, above all else, this first-stage analysis will help guide the scoping for bespoke research and ensure that investment is effectively targeted.

Table 2.1 offers suggestions of where existing insight might be found.

When it comes to bespoke research, a range of methodologies should be considered – traditional focus group discussions, online surveys and virtual focus groups, traditional paper surveys, structured face-to-face and, where necessary, 'at a distance' interviews. Certain talent segments need to be reached through specific methodologies and, in an external setting,

Table 2.1   Potential information sources for existing insight

Information type	Potential Source
Employee engagement – regulated measurement	Employee engagement survey Employee recognition schemes Cultural practices around good news and bad news Customer service surveys (which include observations on employee behaviour) Exit interviews Any union-led opinion surveys on aspects of employment and/or organisational change Any cultural survey/assessment work
Employer attitudes – formal communication	Materials audit – covering all aspects of communication across the employee lifecycle, for example, offer letter, induction, performance review and so on. Internal communications – materials, channels and feedback Communication of corporate goals and so on (vision values and so on.) Candidate experience audit Candidate behaviours/feedback (both directly and through third-party suppliers) Employee acquisition and retention data by skills group/roles Corporate communications which refer to employee issues Human capital reports Annual reports CSR reports Diversity research and initiatives which capture attitudes and views
Employee engagement – unregulated feedback	Any 'published' views from 'brand cynics and saboteurs' – blogs, networking sites and so on.

typically need incentivising to take part. The outcome of this phase should be a clear understanding of what the key perceptions of the organisation as an employer are – viewed from both inside and outside – and the key drivers behind those views, analysed across a number of dimensions. This is essential not only for segmentation, but also for appreciating the way in which different aspects of the 'employee deal' play out for different groups.

As mentioned earlier, Chapter 3 offers more detail on the employee lifecycle and the concept of touchpoints. A core output of doing the right kind of research should be a better understanding of the moments of truth for the employee experience within the organisation. Good engagement research should always produce this, but does not always go as far as eliciting the symbols, language and stories which are so often associated with these.

STAGE 3: PROPOSITION DEVELOPMENT AND TESTING

Core Activities	Core Outputs
Development of employee value proposition based on research outcomes and customer proposition/corporate brand alignment	Employee value proposition Sub-value propositions as required Creative interpretation if relevant
Validation	

This is the point at which the insight gained through the research phase is balanced against the aspirations for the brand as an employer and the EVP is defined. It would be normal to develop an overarching EVP for an organisation but, at the same time, acknowledge that sub-EVPs can exist for different parts and/or different segments. The key is the 'golden thread' which links them.

This is also where there can be an interesting challenge, depending on the organisation's existing brand architecture. This is picked up by Annette Frem (Chapter 3) when she considers the challenge of multiple brand environments. Some organisations need to ask themselves whether they are a 'house of brands' – a holding company sitting behind the brand portfolio – or are leading with a 'master brand' and therefore are a 'branded house'. This is, of course, not the only question of brand alignment. The deal with the customer/consumer has to be in harmony with that with the employees, and there are stakeholders to consider, too. As demonstrated by our brand model in Chapter 1 there are, of course, other brand audiences to bear in mind, as well as the need to be aware of the balance with shareholder communication. Deals cannot be made with customers or employees that cannot be sold to shareholders!

EVP development is a challenging exercise for anyone – whether it is an organisation working on its own or a partnership between supplier and organisation. It is the point at which science meets art and an articulation is developed that aims to capture both the rational and emotional aspects of the employee deal. So often, propositions fail on three fronts: capturing the two-way aspect of the employee deal, being distinctive and being compelling. We would encourage an element of aspiration to any proposition development – whilst not everyone joins an organisation to 'save the planet', everyone is seeking something – even if the aspiration is a better work–life balance. The trick is tap into this emotional dimension, underpinned by the reality of the deal as validated by the research.

We would recommend that draft propositions be developed and then validated. Inside the organisation, it would be acceptable to go back to a group selected from the initial internal research audience. To use identified research participants for a second time is perfectly acceptable from a research integrity perspective. In fact, we have found that this approach is helpful because these people should already have an understanding about where an 'EVP' fits in and what it is based on, and avoids having to resell the exercise to a fresh set of participants. Externally there is an argument for 'fresh eyes', but an economic solution would be to ask the original participants if they are happy to be contacted at a later date to test the outputs.

A key question is precisely what is being validated? Simple words or creative interpretations to bring a proposition to life? The purist would suggest that in the first instance the pure articulation needs to be tested. The problem with this approach is that this does not reflect how we consume any brand, let alone an employer brand. We don't 'judge' the BMW brand on the words 'ultimate driving machine'; we judge BMW on the driving experience of our chosen product. This is why the use of communication samples is useful and therefore creative interpretation plays its part. However, we need to issue a health warning here. All too often creative judgement takes over the proposition validation, resulting in the exercise becoming a design brief and not an articulation of something which is fundamentally cultural and should be guiding behaviours just as much as, if not more than, it guides creative messaging.

STAGE 4: IMPLEMENTATION

Core Activities	Core Outputs
EVP impact analysis – linked to touchpoint mapping	Roll out plan with touchpoint priorities
	Communication toolkits
	User workshops

Thoughts about implementation should not be new at this stage. Defining this would be part of the initial 'visioning' phase, but in our experience ideas about implementation can change through the course of researching and defining an employer brand. Consequently, anyone embarking on the journey should be aware of this. Opportunities and requirements emerge to do things differently and to make a statement about the positioning of the brand through the use of experiential marketing, particularly to the internal stakeholder audience who, by definition, are the group who need to own and be motivated by the outcomes of the whole exercise. Insight also emerges on attraction and retention, and therefore deployment activities need to be sufficiently flexible to accommodate this. It is likely that, numerous organisational implications will arise at the proposition development stage – they can range from leadership and reward to simple process changes, but they are all aspects of how the organisation will 'prove' its promise to its people.

Some of the aspects of the employee lifecycle to consider are detailed in Chapter 3, p. 51.

STAGE 5: MEASUREMENT

Core Activities	Core Outputs
Measurement programme based on agreed ROI measures	Employer brand scorecard
Links to other brand and reputation measurement programmes	

Measuring the success of employer brand projects is challenging because an employer brand is a journey. However, we think it is essential that every effort is made to set ROI objectives at the outset.

At this point we are not going to go into detail about this stage as we have devoted Chapter 11 to the question of measurement and a suggested employer brand scorecard.

However, for the sake of completion, here are a number of success measures that organisations can consider – some perhaps 'softer' than others:

- improved employee engagement measures;

- advocacy of the organisation as an employer;

- internal awareness and identification with the employer brand;

- consistent use of the brand guidelines for communications across a range of channels – both internally and externally;

- improved attraction metrics;

- improved retention metrics.

Summary

Many other books have devoted entire sections to cover what we have set out in a single chapter here. But in the process they have not offered up a clear definition of what the employer brand is and what some of the confusing jargon used in conjunction with it really means.

The five-step methodology is based on a classic brand development model. It is not a one-off exercise. Once defined, brands need managing, and they evolve. However, embarking on brand definition in this way is no guarantee of future-proofing your employer brand. In fact, deciding to manage your brand as an employer should be viewed as a way of organisational life – an element of your strategic behaviours, as opposed to a project which will suddenly provide a panacea to a number of people problems.

3

Engagement – The Power of People

Annette Frem
Bernard Hodes Group

Why is the people asset suddenly such a hot topic? And why should employer branding be considered anything more than a communications exercise in producing pretty pictures?

In this chapter we'll elaborate on the answers we've already given to these two fundamental questions. We have already touched on the influence of corporate branding and the realisation that the way employees behave when interacting with customers, suppliers, and shareholders is a key differentiating factor for companies in every market.

What's more, we've started to examine the far-reaching impact of the war for talent. We've seen how the low birthrate in the late 1980s has combined with an ageing workforce to create a worldwide skills shortage, which is helping to foster a different mindset amongst the new generations entering the world of work. Conventional working culture is being challenged as never before, and work–life balance has come to the fore.

Now we're going to take a closer look at some of the other issues that have given questions about human capital and talent pools unprecedented coverage on boardroom agendas. And, in the process, we hope to show why managing your organisation's employer brand has to be at the heart of your HR and/or people strategy.

The Psychological Contract and Engagement

Helen Rosethorn argued in Chapter 2 that the 'engagement' word had overtaken the psychological contract concept because of its perceived clearer link to improved productivity and organisational success. Let's take a closer look at the literature around both topics and discuss why it is relevant in regards to employer branding.

DEFINING ENGAGEMENT

Definitions of employee engagement abound, and there are as many versions as there are academics and consultants working in this field. The literature is legion, although the most respected commentators do have elements in common.

Below are the three dimensions that most seem to agree on. These are included with some of the key engagement levers that the CIPD and Institute of Employment Studies have found through extensive research:[1]

1. *The emotional or affective dimension.* What do your employees feel about you as a company? Is there an emotional 'bond' between them and you, and does it make them proud to work for you? Would they recommend you to friends and family as a preferred company to work for?

    Key levers:

    •   I feel my company is concerned about my health and well-being.

    •   I feel I'm enabled to perform well.

    •   I feel well informed about what is happening in my company.

---

1   The description of the three elements is from ISR's 'Engagement White Paper, 'Creating Competitive Advantage from your Employees: A Global Study of Employee Engagement', http://www.isrinsight.co, and the description of the engagement levers and main components are from page 2 of the 'CIPD Employee Engagement January 2007' paper, http:// www. peopleresources:ie/cipd-employee-engagement.pdf, and from D. Robinson, H. Hooker and S. Hayday, *Engagement: The Continued Story*, Report 447, Institute for Employment Studies, London, p. 29.

2.   *The cognitive dimension.* What do your employees think about you as a company? Is there an intellectual 'fit' between them and you? Do they believe in the vision, business strategy and objectives, and do they agree and support the company's values?

Key levers:

- I believe my manager is committed to the company.

- I can express my ideas freely, and management listens.

3.   *The behavioural or physical dimension.* How do your employees behave? Are they willing to go the extra mile, giving you discretionary effort, and do they want to stay with you?

Key levers:

- I'm involved in decision-making.

- I can influence my job.

Naturally, these three dimensions can't be seen in isolation from the external and internal environment – a point we will come back to when talking about holistic brand management.

The key point is that people today have more of a choice. Employees choose whether or not to be engaged, and employers need to find out what their unique engagement triggers are. Employers need to tick more boxes than ever to be 'awarded' with employees' engagement.

It's tempting to say that when employees are proud to work for you (Dimension 1) and believe in your vision and business strategy (Dimension 2), then that is what drives that discretionary effort and willingness to stay (Dimension 3).

Interestingly, this view seems to be shared by the Corporate Leadership Council which has a simpler model of engagement which works with rational and emotional engagement:

Emotional commitment is defined as the extent to which employees derive pride, enjoyment, inspiration or meaning from something or

someone in the organization. While rational commitment is defined as
the extent to which employees feel that someone or something within
their organizations provides financial, developmental, or professional
rewards that are in their best interests.[2]

Two companies spring to mind when talking about rational and emotional
commitment and how this thinking can be integrated into employer
propositions.

Orange UK recently divided its proposition into two main parts, giving
them the headings 'heart' and 'mind', and Virgin is equally explicit in its use
of rational and emotional terms. Virgin Mobile calls its parts of the employer
proposition 'Head' and 'Heart'.

Some of the employee engagement levers unearthed in the Leadership
Council's findings are particularly interesting in the context of employer
branding. The Council claims that employee retention occurs when employees
believe that there is something in it for them, although there is an important
caveat to this – namely, you don't get employees to go the extra mile unless
they believe in what they do, their team and their organisation. This finding
supports the argument that sparked the trend of organisations moving from
measuring employee satisfaction to measuring engagement. It was noted that
employees might be satisfied, but it didn't necessarily mean that they did a
great job and wanted to go that extra mile. It was only if you could turn them
from being satisfied to being engaged that you would get that sought-after
discretionary effort.

The Leadership Council's research also expands on the understanding of
the immediate manager's role in employee engagement. The findings claim
that the focus of the manager's role should be as a key influencer and enabler
of the employee's commitment to the job, business and colleagues. The
emphasis is on the leader's role as a communicator, and this is supported by
some of the leading communication theories, which emphasise how stories
are fundamental to human existence – for example, that we construct our
understanding of the world with the stories we tell[3] and are told. Some of our

---

2   Corporate Executive Board, 'The Corporate Leadership Council: Driving Performance and
    Retention through Employee Engagement' 2004, p. 9 at: http://www.lloydmorgan.com/PDF/
    Driving%20Performance%20and%20Retention%20Through%20Employee%20Engagement.
    pdf.
3   Inspired by Gregory Bateson's views on communication theories in Nano McCaughan and
    Barry Palmer, *Systems Thinking for Harassed Managers*, Karmac Books, London, 1994.

most ingrained beliefs and cultural values, such as the difference between right and wrong, are communicated from generation to generation by stories. Indeed, the research's highlighting of the importance of communication reflects the growth of story-telling both as a strategic tool and as a fundamental leadership skill.

The third and most important driver of engagement corresponds with the cognitive component that we highlighted earlier. The better employees understand how their day-to-day job contributes to business strategy and business success, the more engaged they will be.

An interesting and very public example of this was displayed in Jamie Oliver's TV documentary *Jamie's School Dinners*, in which we followed Jamie's attempts to persuade children to eat fresh, tasty nutritious meals instead of junk food. It became clear very quickly that the mindset of the dinner ladies was one of the key challenges to tackle. Through various techniques, interventions and careful coaching, the 'dinner ladies' learned that they played a significant role in the educational system. Nutritious food gives children the ability to sit still and concentrate for longer and enhances their ability to learn, and, as a result, dinner ladies play a key role in bringing these benefits to life. As the programme showed, the breakthrough came when the dinner ladies understood what Jamie was trying to achieve and how their job could, and did, make a huge difference to countless children every day.

So the consensus is that employee engagement is the result of a well-designed strategy, where all the components play a role in their own right, but, when put together, add up to more than the sums of the parts.

Through our research and work around employee engagement, employer reputation and brand perception over the last seven years, we have refined our thinking about what we see as the key components of employee engagement. Figure 3.1 depicts the engagement model that we use in Hodes when working with global and local employers to understand their employer reputation. (We'll look at this in more detail in Chapter 11.)

THE PSYCHOLOGICAL CONTRACT

As with engagement, the psychological contract has been the focus for many different academics and practitioners. Professor Graeme Martin's summary

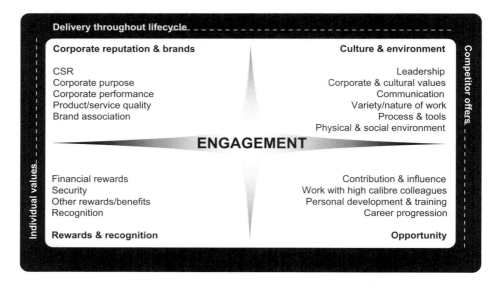

Figure 3.1   Key components of employee engagement

of Thompson and Bunderson's thoughts on the three different types of psychological contract is the basis for our discussion.[4]

The first of the three types of contracts he identifies is the transactional type. This is a traditional employer–employee deal of the industrial age, which was modified by unions throughout Europe in the late 1970s. It's best characterised as 'a fair day's work for a fair day's pay – and a fair degree of job security and occupational safety'.

A new type of contract emerged in the latter part of the twentieth century, as the industrial economies became more service-based. (Of course, this evolution is far from complete in many emerging markets and, as we shall discuss later, this affects what employees in different parts of the world are looking for from employers.) This new type of contract was much more relational. It meant that employees were willing to '[g]o beyond their contract by doing excellent work and demonstrating high commitment and identification with the organisation' if they felt the conditions were right. They had to see that they would receive in return 'a career with training and education, promotion opportunities, interesting work and long-term employment prospects'.[5]

---

4   Graeme Martin, *Managing People and Organisations in Changing Contexts*, Butterworth-Heinemann, Oxford, 2006.
5   Ibid., p. 76.

As already touched on, this shift in employees' mindsets corresponded with organisations' realisation that human capital was the differentiating part in their corporate branding efforts, and it also reflected the emergence of Generation X and their need for constant learning and development opportunities.

Over the last 10–15 years another psychological contract seems to have emerged. Once again, the core of the deal is aligned with the changes we see in modern society and the increased focus on shared social responsibility. This third type of contract is called 'the ideological contract'. Here the two-way deal is that employees are willing to '[p]articipate fully in the organisational mission/cause by being a good organisational and societal citizen' in exchange for the organisation 'demonstrating credible commitment to a valued cause'.[6] This type of contract is aligned with some of Generation Y's key values. Interestingly, it is also very much in tune with the basis of corporate branding – in which an organisation's mission creates an emotional bond between the company and its employees and customers.

Whether the change in society pre-dated the change in the collective mindset is a chicken-and-egg discussion which we are not going to settle here. However, the changing nature of contracts is a consideration for those organisations that are embarking on an employer brand journey. Companies need to take care to build employee propositions with a sufficiently wide appeal to engage every group in their workforce, whether they are attracted by an ideological, relational or more transactional contract. The challenge is to engage baby-boomers as well as Generations X and Y, which is why the notion of segmentation and employee subpropositions discussed in Chapter 2 is so central to Hodes's approach.

Competing Theories, Complementary Values

Engagement and the psychological contract have developed in parallel to describe employee behaviour and commitment. Whilst both have their virtues, the concept of engagement is arguably more productively applied to employer branding discussions because it offers not only a good explanation of discretionary effort, but also a better starting-point for organisations to address the diverse expectations of their people. That said, here at Hodes we believe that the theory of the psychological contract has made a useful contribution to explaining employee behaviour and is an integral strand in the origin of

---

6   Ibid.

the employer brand. Moreover, we believe the phrasing of the relationship between employers and employees as a contract is a valuable insight and we've expanded on this approach in our positioning of the employer brand journey as an employee deal.

Managing the Deal

The basis of the Hodes philosophy is that the employer brand is a two-way deal between employees and employers, and the right balance needs to be struck between the expectations on both sides. Figure 3.2 illustrates the different component parts of the deal.

In Figure 3.2, on one side of the balance is your proposition as a company – for example, your unique selling points communicated as an compelling story about what employees and potential employees can expect from you as a company. It is not only what you have to offer, but also what you would be prepared to 'pay' to attract and keep the people you want. (This is illustrated by our engagement model – Figure 3.1 – because your unique engagement drivers

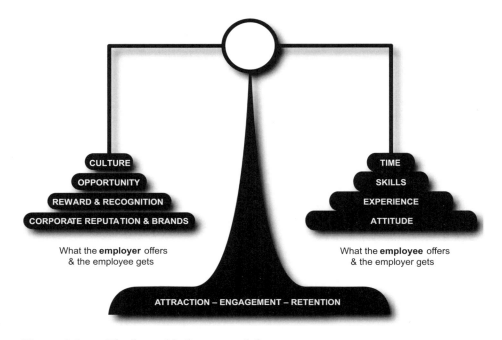

Figure 3.2   The brand balance model

should be the building-blocks of your proposition.) On the other side is the employee with his or her experience, attitude, skill-set and time. This is what they have to offer, but also the price they are willing to 'pay' for coming to work for you and staying with you.

Naturally, where the balance is set will be influenced by employees' perceptions of their own marketability, and it will be interesting to see how the changing economic climate will affect the two sides of the equation. However, the important point is that organisations should always strive to get the balance right – creating a win–win situation where both parties feel they have done a good deal.

It is also important to acknowledge that the deal needs to be constantly renegotiated as the organisation grows and employees join, develop and leave. It is worth remembering that every time you, as an organisation, hire a new employee you are not only negotiating the tangible aspects of the employment deal, such as pay and benefits, but also negotiating intangible and implicit considerations. These include such questions as: 'Do I like the product and service, the vision, the culture and the environment?' and 'What do I get out of joining your organisation in return for my time and my commitment?'

Before deciding to join an organisation, employees will take in clues about what's on offer from a myriad different sources. Later in this chapter we will look at how organisations can manage these expectations more effectively.

In Times of Change

The year 2007 was considered the peak of the recent extended cycle or wave of mergers and acquisitions (M&As). The market has changed since then, although businesses are still driven by the same factors: the need to build market share, the development of their service portfolio, the refinement of their customer offering and the need to keep innovating.

During M&As, consolidations and spin-offs, HR is traditionally busy providing due diligence about the changes to the workforce and the value of intellectual capital. Elsewhere, their colleagues in Marketing and Product Development are busy trialling potential corporate propositions with customers, asking hard questions about the future of the organisation's products. What services do customers like best? What attributes do they associate with the product and the company? And how likely are they to continue buying the products? This means that HR is potentially losing out on addressing an even more pressing issue: identifying and managing the current and future brand engagement drivers of the critical talent mass and wider employee population.

Many commentators identify culture and leadership as the key reasons why some M&As become huge success stories and others fall short. The reason for failure is often traced back to a leadership style that doesn't translate successfully between cultures. But, in our judgement, this is only a partial truth. Whilst leaders and their approach will have a huge impact on the success of an M&A – a point we'll pick up again later in this chapter – we also believe that, in some cases, the foundation for success (or failure) is laid long before the M&A is even announced. This means that only careful insight, understanding and management of the reputations of the different organisations involved, and the 'deals' they hold with their employees, will ensure a successful outcome.

There are, therefore, some key priorities for organisations completing mergers or acquisitions. They need to remain focused on being seen as an attractive destination for the talent. They need to work hard to ensure that they don't lose key talent in the process. And, last but not least, they need to keep the wider workforce engaged before during and after the M&A, making sure that the 'value profit chain' is kept intact.[7]

REPUTATION: A HELP OR A HINDRANCE?

As we argued in Chapter 2, your brand has different audiences, each of which have a different relationship to your organisation. Until now, we have split the employee segment into current employees and potential employees. However, when we talk about the employer brand in the context of M&As there is an added element. Suddenly, you need to consider the needs and expectations of an employee group that hasn't actively decided to be part of your company.

This employee group will now be the focus of our attention, although we will also touch on the employees in the acquiring company not least

---

7   On the jacket of J.L. Heskett, W.E. Sasser, and L.A. Schlesinger, *The Value Profit Chain*, Harvard Business School Publishing, Boston, MA, 2003, the 'value profit chain' is described as 'a quantifiable set of associations' involving treating employees like customers and customers like employees: 'today's employee satisfaction, loyalty, and commitment strongly influences tomorrow's customer satisfaction, loyalty, and commitment and ultimately the organisation's profit and growth.'

because the attitude and behaviours of these two groups will determine the scale and nature of the challenge which HR and Internal Communications is facing.

Let's start by identifying the different situations in which acquiring brands can find themselves:

1. *The acquiring brand is less/not known – neutral connotations.*
   It is worth remembering that employer reputation is relative. Often the best-known brands in their market – well-established local utilities, for instance – are unknown outside their sphere of influence. And so the major partner in a merger or acquisition may come to the deal with little or no brand equity, from an employee perspective, What's more, corporate behaviour and cultural norms can easily be misinterpreted when the two employee groups are relatively unknown to each other.

2. *The acquiring brand is well known – holds positive connotations.*
   If your organisation is a global success and has high brand awareness (think Apple, Google and so on), then you enter a merger or acquisition from a position of strength. You can assume that employees in the acquired company will know you and that their perception of you as an employer will be positive. And if they don't hold a positive perception of their current company as an employer, then negotiating a new 'deal' with them could be fairly straightforward. You will, of course, have a bigger challenge on your hands if they hold a positive perception of their current employer as well and need to be persuaded of what the acquiring brand can provide over and above their current deal.

3. *The acquiring brand is well known – negative connotations.*
   At the other end of the spectrum, the acquiring brand may operate in a poorly perceived industry – arms, tobacco or oil, for instance – or it may have some CSR or employee relations issues. If this is the case, it approaches the merger or acquisition from a weaker position. From an employee perspective, you can assume that willingness to renegotiate the deal is potentially very small and that a big effort will have to go into explaining, reassuring and communicating the benefits of change. The quality of management is a key consideration here – a theme to which we'll return.

Forewarned is Forearmed

Regardless of whether employees in the acquired company hold a positive perception of their current company or not, the important point is to understand these perceptions. You need to know and understand the current employer brand proposition. What is the 'deal' that employees have signed up to and how does it differ from the new 'deal' on the table? Only by finding the answer to this will you understand what your challenges are and how you need to plan and execute the appropriate change process to achieve a successful long-term relationship.

Naturally, this is often easier said than done. Most M&As are driven by changes in the industry, the opportunity to make cost efficiencies and global expansion plans. Employee interests often come a poor second in these circumstances. The interests of the other brand audiences – customers, shareholders and governments – are normally paramount for most executive teams. And many of these teams will find their discussions and decisions about corporate and employer brands are taking place in an environment in which management status, board room politics and intercompany rivalries are playing out day to day.

THE PEOPLE POSSIBILITIES OF CHANGE

Naturally, different business strategies call for different talent agendas and sourcing plans. The right people now might not be the right people for tomorrow. And, in times of change, such as during mergers and acquisitions, organisations need to ask themselves far-reaching questions about what sort of behaviours they need to encourage and support to secure their future.

A sector that has asked itself these questions in recent years is the charitable and not-for-profit one. The market has become saturated as the number of charities has grown and the fight for government funding and public support has intensified. In turn, this has changed the profile of the people that charities are looking for. In simple terms, the key requirement used to be a big heart; now, commercial acumen, customer focus and, often, a talent for government lobbying have moved to the top of the wish-list.

Other organisations are also facing this scenario. Before the advent of the Internet, the travel industry had the advantage that individuals were unable to purchase and negotiate good direct deals on flight tickets, accommodation and so on. Now people can plan and book their travel directly online and don't have to interact with a travel agent at all. Under threat as never before, the travel industry was forced to take a good hard look at itself and define what difference it could make in the eyes of the customer. Being in the service industry, many travel agencies have picked up on the point made earlier 'that staff behaviours are the embodiment of the brand' and have used that as the differentiating factor.

When your industry changes, your business strategy changes and you have an opportunity to change the company's proposition. This is clearly a pivotal point in the development of any organisation. And, from an employer branding perspective, it's imperative that no decision about future directions are reached without proper debate about the consequences to attract and retain key talent and maintain critical employee mass.

House of Brands versus Branded House

We've found that the models shown in Figures 3.3 and 3.4 help HR and Internal Communications practitioners understand their current business and branding strategy. They are useful tools for demonstrating how proposed changes play out and what the associated implications for brand perception, attractiveness and engagement could be. (We've applied the same models in order to understand global mergers in Chapter 4.)

A 'House of Brands' (Figure 3.3) is when you have a corporate brand proposition and standalone entities operating under separate brands. For example, The Royal Bank of Scotland Group is the corporate brand; Natwest, Churchill, Direct Line, Privilege, Citizenbank and so on are standalone entities. HBOS is the corporate brand; Halifax, Esure, rightmove.co.uk, Sainsbury's bank and so on are standalone entities. Similarly, Premier Travel Inns, Costa Coffee and Beefeater are standalone brands under the Whitbread umbrella. And the luxury goods group LVMH comprises the standalone brands Thomas Pink, Moet Hennessy and Louis Vuitton.

In the world of product branding, this sort of differentiation would be classified as a corporate brand with sub-brands. There are different reasons for companies choosing to go down the sub-brand route. One reason might be because the company has both a low-value product and a high-value product aimed at different customer segments within the same category. It then has the

Figure 3.3   House of Brands model

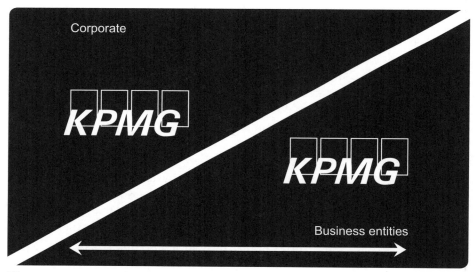

Figure 3.4   Branded House model

problem of differentiating the propositions without undermining what is, after all, a sister brand (think Tesco Value range versus Tesco Finest).

Alternatively, the corporate brand might simply be a holding company, so linking the product to the corporate brand wouldn't bring any value to either the product or the company. Companies pursuing vertical expansion strategies often find themselves in this position (think Kingfisher with Comet and B&Q).

A variation of the Branded House is the endorsed Branded House. Virgin Group, with Virgin Mobile, Virgin Media, Virgin Brides, Virgin Megastores and so on, is a good example of the associations with the corporate brand being viewed to be of value and of benefit to the entities. Here, the organisation celebrates its diversity by adopting a brand strategy that emphasises its expertise in different sectors and underlining this through a consistent approach to naming and corporate identity.

At the opposite end of the spectrum from the House of Brands multi-brand strategy is the single-brand proposition: the Branded House (see Figure 3.4). This is when there is only little or no difference between the corporate and consumer propositions. Examples include STA travel and KPMG.

A single-brand proposition is very common in the service industry where the product is often of a behavioural nature and more or less 'intangible'. For some, it is also a question of size and maturity, since it could be argued that when companies reach a certain size and value they become targets for investment groups or competitors and quickly become part of a House of Brands's portfolio.

The relevance to employer branding is easy to see. As we've already established, brands generate assumptions, expectations and loyalty, and company vision and business strategy are key engagement drivers. This means that a company's decision to be a Branded House or a House of Brands can't be viewed in isolation from the people agenda. An individual can be a customer, employee and shareholder of the same company. So the behaviour a company displays and the employee proposition it adopts will have an influence on its ability to attract and retain the workforce it needs to succeed in the marketplace.

You might be in a situation where you can't attract professionals to your headquarters because potential employees view you as a standalone, high-street brand. The fact that you are a part of a global multi-branded group which could offer interesting career prospects and development opportunities gets lost along the way. Or, of course, you could find yourself at the opposite end of the scale, perceived as a big corporate headquarters that nobody has really heard about, far removed from the line and unable to offer people the opportunity to make a difference to customers.

In times of change, you should invest in solid research aimed at understanding the current perception of your brand(s). Take the time to discover what potential employees know about you and what they think about you as a potential employer. Investigate why your current employees joined and what brand perceptions they might hold of your potential brand portfolio, if indeed yours is a House of Brands. This, as you will almost immediately discover, will be time and effort well spent.

Here at Hodes, we have long experience of completing research into the equity and attractiveness of brands and sub-brands. For example, we've recently helped a major retailer understand how different employee segments (divided along professional lines) were attracted to different brands in the portfolio. The findings were immensely useful. Not only did they help the client understand their employees' engagement drivers, but they also enabled them to tailor their offerings in a much more segmented and targeted way.

The interesting thing is that when comparing budget allocations for consumer research and employee insight, the gap between the two is still staggering. And, unfortunately, these financial disparities reflect the huge gulf in the rigour and science with which organisations approach the related tasks of defining and developing customer and employee propositions. No corporate communication or brand department would launch any product or corporate proposition without undertaking solid market research in order to understand both their customers' needs and the competitor landscape. They spend significant time on defining and investigating the customer's demographic make-up – who they are, where they live, their education, where they work, which newspaper they read and so on. And on the basis of all this knowledge, they segment their audience, build the product value proposition and develop marketing strategies and media planning accordingly. The focus is on maximising the investment – and the returns on investment will be increased brand awareness, successfully stimulated buying behaviours and exceeded sales figures.

As part of the segmentation process and proposition development, product marketers consider every touchpoint on the customer journey – that is, everything that can have an influence on the customer's willingness to buy. They will examine and assess all touchpoints against three key elements of the brand: the tone of voice, the visual look and feel, and the 'behavioural content'. The idea is to make sure that the brand essence is being communicated through each of these touchpoints. This means that they are not only working on developing the product and its packaging, but are extending this to include things like the location of shops, their opening hours, staff numbers, staff uniforms and the quality of facilities such as toilets and waiting areas. Other features considered include queuing systems, staff behaviours, credit card facilities, the product portfolio, stock availability, delivery times, return and refund polities, loyalty schemes, parking and packaging – even the quality of carrier bags comes under scrutiny.

So how much of this approach can be, and is, incorporated into the development of employee propositions? The short answer is: not enough. But first let's look at the thinking as it's applied to the people sphere, so that we can see where the gaps lie.

The fundamentals of the employer branding journey are clearly heavily inspired by the methodology and tools incorporated in brand management. Audience insight and understanding candidate triggers are the starting-points, just as they are in consumer marketing. Indeed, it's only by knowing why your employees are attracted to, and staying with, you that you can discover how to unearth their discretionary effort and engage their commitment.

Applying Brand Management to the People Promise

THE EMPLOYEE LIFECYCLE AND TOUCHPOINTS

The first time we formalised our thinking around touchpoints was when we worked with Philips on their employer brand, which you can read more about in Chapter 5.

There are three stages in an 'employee lifecycle'. The first stage is when you are a candidate, the next stage is when you are an employee and the third and final one is when you are alumni. Each stage of the lifecycle has different touchpoints that you need to manage carefully. The following is a list of where you find the touchpoints relevant for each stage:

- Candidate

    - recruitment marketing strategy and media channels,

    - recruitment process,

    - candidate care,

      –   selection and assessment.

- Employee

  –   introduction and on-boarding process,

  –   culture and leadership behaviours,

  –   training and development,

  –   talent management and career paths,

  –   recognition and rewards,

  –   internal communication,

  –   office space,

  –   compensation and benefits.

- Alumni

  –   exit process,

  –   redundancy policies and packages,

  –   alumni networks.

Touchpoints can be any internal tool, process, environmental feature or policy that touches a candidate/employee/alumni, and any employer branding exercise should identify, audit and assess key touchpoints against the desired proposition. What's more, the ongoing development and adjustment of touchpoints should be seen as a key and continuous responsibility of the HR department.

Touchpoints that do not deliver on the promises rooted in your proposition run the risk of failing to deliver on basic, but potentially crucial, expectations. And the effects of this are never positive. Withdrawn applications, turned-down offers and disengaged employees are the most common consequences of failing to deliver through the day-to-day experience that candidates/employees have with you.

THE THREE KEY DIMENSIONS

As discussed, there are three key dimensions to a touchpoint.

1. The look and feel

The look and feel is about the basic visual elements of traditional branding. It's about font, colour, image, style and use of logos. It's about the use of visual iconography to create recognition and elicit an emotional reaction.

I think we have all experienced situations where the 'look and feel' didn't match what a company was trying to encourage us to believe about them, either as customers or as employees: the upmarket hotel with dirty, nylon sheets; the exclusive car-hire firm that leaves cigarette butts in the ashtray. Examples abound of where the look and feel of the customer experience didn't match the brand promise. The damage to brands in these moments of truth is lasting. The trust disappears in an instant, and the best-planned customer and employer propositions immediately evaporate to be replaced with employee and customer frustration and disappointment.

Naturally, it's not only the 'look' which is important – the feel of brand communication and experiences is a vital consideration, too. In the world of HR communications, the quality of the paper you print your graduate communication on or the strength of the binders you produce for internal training programmes can be as important as the food that you serve in the canteen. They are all implicit carriers of your proposition as an employer and act as moments of revelation.

A quick simple test is to take whatever material (a brochure, a recruitment ad or a poster for a Refer a Friend scheme) you are auditing and put your hand over the logo. Is the material unmistakably yours, or could it be from any company in the world? Remember, the first time you set foot in your reception area? What did this suggest about the business you were just about to visit and how much of this has turned out to be true?

2. The tone of voice

Tone of voice is summed up in the familiar phase 'It's not what you say, but how you say it'. Your 'tone of voice' is made up of the words you choose to use in all your communication.

It's about how you speak to people. Think about the language you use as an organisation. Do you refer to staff or people, graduates or future talent, factory workers or production agents? And in external communications and correspondence about you as an employer, what do you call yourself? Do you use 'we' or 'the company', 'subsidiaries' or 'business units'?

If your proposition encourages an informal tone of voice and you emphasise openness and trust in the organisation, it's important that you use words which reflect this. For example, a 25-page expenses policy written in legalese could make the company appear like a mistrusting parent rather than a thoughtful employer.

3. Behavioural content

This is the most complicated area, but it's important to get right. This is about delivering on your promises as a company and rewarding and recognising people for displaying the behaviours you would like to see. The secret of doing this is to look at the way in which key programmes and tools are structured.

Many companies over the years have spent significant time on identifying best practice, either internally or externally, and invested time and money on deploying this knowledge throughout the organisation. However, organisations should ask themselves whether that particular way of doing things is true to their proposition. More specifically, they need to assess whether their way of working develops, rewards and recognises the behaviours that are key to them as a company and which display their cultural and organisational values.

For example, imagine you are trying to support a new business proposition that focuses on the commercial awareness and capabilities of your people. How can you make sure that your internal touchpoints identify, develop, train, reward and recognise these kinds of behaviours?

Does your behavioural framework, which supports recruitment processes and assessment centres, emphasise commercial behaviours? Do you assess employee behaviour as part of your performance management processes? Are your bonus and/or commission schemes linked to sales targets and overall company performance? Do your company's recognition schemes reward and recognise commercial awareness? Does your induction programme include sales training and is the emphasis placed on it proportional to its importance to your company? Are sales figures, forecasts and customer satisfaction scores made available and shared with employees? Are employee engagement scores linked to branch/division performance and customer satisfaction and retention? Do the stories in your internal magazines demonstrate employees going out of their way to ensure customer satisfaction?

Clearly, there are a myriad ways in which behaviours can bring your proposition to life The key point is to ensure that each touchpoint is telling the same story.

Failing to get your touchpoints right can have an unexpected impact on the return on your investments in your recruitment communication and engagement efforts. For instance, a mismatch between attraction and assessment techniques can lead to huge wastage in recruitment campaigns and unnecessary administration, as the wrong sort of candidates enter the process.

The clearer your employer brand and employee value proposition is, the more tangible and concrete you can make the discussion around the 'deal'. Crucially, you can then manage and meet expectations first raised in the recruitment process and then later in internal stages of the employee journey.

The following example nicely illustrates the impact of the corporate brand proposition on engagement.

For many years I worked in a niche travel agency, whose target audience was young people and students wanting to take a sabbatical and backpack around the world. The company's unique selling point was that the agents sitting behind the counter in the branches were the spitting image of the customers. This encouraged customers to trust the adviser's advice and tips, as they could identify closely with them.

The consumer proposition was communicated very clearly and dramatically in customer materials, showing a cartoon figure on a timeline developing from an infant to a child to a young adult, then 'falling over' when they reach 33. The proposition was brought to life in the strap line, 'Go before it's too late', which figured on all customer and corporate communication.

This very public statement led to both candidates and employees asking, 'Will I get fired when I turn 33?' The answer was, of course, 'No'. Nevertheless there was an expectation in the business that people would only remain in front-line roles for between one and half and three years. It was assumed that people would want to go travelling again, start their studies or take up a back-office job after that length of time. This openness around expectations was welcomed by everyone. Employees knew the score when it came to development and career prospects and were able to integrate the role into their other life plans. Equally, the openness helped the company with resource planning and enabled them to map out the investment they needed to make in the individual.

This example highlights how a more holistic view of the relationship between a company's consumer and employee propositions can influence HR thinking and drive open and productive conversations around the deal, which in turn builds engagement.

4

Globalisation – Considerations for the Journey

Annette Frem and Helen Rosethorn
Bernard Hodes Group

Readers may be tempted to skip this chapter, but global considerations should be of interest to everyone exploring the concept of employer branding – even if you believe that your own brand is purely 'local'.

Why? Because, as we explained in Chapter 1, thinking globally is high on the agenda for some organisations as they expand into new territories – whether organically or through merger and acquisition – but for others it is simply about the battlefronts of the war for talent and these are increasingly global. Organisations can be tapping into new markets for labour beyond their shores simply to plug the gaps in the labour markets at home.

This chapter will set out what we believe to be the key considerations when defining, developing and managing employer brands in a global setting – all illustrated with specific examples from the raft of work we have delivered in this sphere.

In our experience there are five golden rules that underpin employer brands which successfully deliver on a global stage:

1.   The starting position of the brand is clearly mapped and understood – and, where it is not clear, time is taken and investment made to make the appropriate assessment.

2.   A common language is used – securing a shared definition for 'employer branding'.

3.   The purpose of defining and managing the brand is clear. Is it purely about recruitment or is it more about a greater alignment of the employee experience across the geography of the organisation?

4.   The organisation's parent culture doesn't have a disproportionate influence on the cultural balance of the business.

5.   The right balance between global and local is determined by the end-goal

Of course, having read the first three chapters of our book, it is very possible to argue that the first four of these 'rules' are relevant for any branding journey. They are, however, thrown to the top of the agenda when different cultures and different stages of brand recognition come into play for the organisation.

Our engagement model in Chapter 3 highlighted the areas that we believe companies need to manage in order to deliver greater employee advocacy and, as a result, discretionary effort. The challenge in a global context is, of course, that what works in one culture could have the exact opposite effect in another culture. We were discussing this with a client who has recently moved to Asia. We were talking about recognition programmes and we both agreed that the European way of celebrating couldn't be more different from that of our colleagues in Africa and Asia. In our eyes, their celebrations seem to be extremely colourful and 'loud', while European celebrations appear very formal and boring.

As this example shows, when building a global employer brand it's important to focus on the *desired outcome* because the route to get there may vary from culture to culture.

Nobody who embarks on an employer brand journey starts with a blank piece of paper. The business (or businesses if we are talking about mergers and acquisitions) comes to the party complete with heritage, cultural origins, stories, ways of working and, perhaps most importantly, senior management's vision for where the company needs to be in the future. It's critical for any practitioner to unravel and understand this complexity in order to plan the journey and identify, and prepare for, any obstacles that might emerge on the way.

Organisations need to understand what it is that they are doing well that made them what they are today and what might have to change to achieve global success. They also need to understand what needs to be added when moving into other countries to ensure resonance and succeed locally. In fact, you could express this path as: local brand goes global, goes local again.

Many organisations ask us if it is possible to have an overarching proposition across countries when we know that different engagement drivers come out on top in global engagement research. On the basis of our experience, we strongly believe that it is possible because, as we've seen, all aspects of the engagement model need to be managed, even if the emphasis on the different elements might vary over time and from country to country.

The aim should always be to look for the highest common factor instead of the lowest common denominator globally. Ideally, organisations should work towards a core proposition that is sufficiently aspirational to engage a multifaceted audience and realistic enough to win local trust.

We have argued for championing the role of research and insight in the building of an employer brand positioning. Now we will expand the argument and explain why this becomes even more important when developing and managing your employer brand on a global scale.

The Starting Position

One of the most important things we have learnt from working with big global players like Philips, Nokia and France Telecom is: never assume anything. Because even though these companies have been playing on the global stage for more than a decade, they all display behaviours which are rooted in the context of their national cultural origins. These need to be uncovered and evaluated to see whether they will help or hinder the company in becoming a more successful global employer.

What businesses have to remember is that their reputation as an employer is often entwined with their development as a business and the product or services that they offer to the public. However, when moving into new territories, the brand doesn't necessarily carry all that information with it. New audiences might not know, understand or appreciate the heritage and past achievements that a business might have found invaluable to date and have worked firmly in its favour.

Needless to say, no audience is comfortable with a gap in their perceptions. In the absence of 'fact', audiences will use other information to inform their perceptions of a brand. From our experience of researching brands worldwide we have found that one particular tendency is to form a view based either on the brand's country of origin or on its name or names associated with it.

Many years ago we were researching the perceptions of the newly formed (but eventually doomed) Marconi organisation. In places like Germany, Marconi was thought to be an American organisation and perceptions of how it operated as an employer were based purely on this view of its roots. The expectation was that they would 'hire and fire' and not necessarily offer the security of employment that other – supposedly better understood – competitors would. In Italy the name had power – drawing on the power of Marconi himself as the father of the telecoms industry.

Those organisations that have a country featured in their name face a particular challenge on their global journey, depending on the territories to be covered and the passage of time. Organisations like British American Tobacco (BAT) were once admired as they expanded around the world for the declared origins in their name. Today, coupled with the issues around the sector in which they operate, research we carried out in 2008 shows that the provenance has significantly less appeal even in countries and regions where tobacco as an industry is accepted.

Sector perceptions are particularly interesting. More developed nations have certain views of roles and their appeal and value in organisational life. As brands travel from the traditional more developed nations to the emerging markets, we need to be very careful about taking these stereotypical views with us. Orange found that when it opened their call centres in territories like the Ivory Coast, the chance to work in these call centres was hugely appealing to well-educated graduates. The brand, the roles, the 'Western' organisation with potential career routes outside Africa – all these features combined to create a very positive perception of the deal with Orange and to catapult it to the most desirable of employer brands on the west coast of Africa.

'Forget assumptions; embrace research' is the conclusion if you are looking to accurately map out your brand's starting-point. And at this point it is worth stressing the need for good, independent research. The way in which research is completed in a global setting speaks volumes about an organisation's commitment to understanding and defining a global employer brand. Research methodologies have to be carefully tailored and developed. Survey questions need to reflect cultural sensitivities. Research channels need to be appropriate to local needs. And translations should be piloted and tested before they are adopted wholesale.

Time invested in fine-tuning research methodologies is always time well spent. In 2008 we completed a global research programme amongst 35,000 employees within a global workforce of 70,000. We found ourselves spending some time taking Japanese stakeholders within the organisation through the structure of our survey tool. In particular, we debated the appropriateness of survey questions with them, not least because they had recently carried out their own engagement survey. When our survey went live, we were delighted that the best response rate worldwide came from Japanese employees.

A Common Language

Creating a common language is a key priority when you're engaged in global employer branding projects. It's very easy to forget that English isn't necessarily everybody's first language, even if it is the chosen language of business. It's also very important to remember that words – indeed, entire concepts – aren't understood in precisely the same way by everyone involved in a project. We discovered this when we were tasked with developing a global recognition scheme some years ago. We surveyed colleagues around the world about what recognition schemes they had in place and received some very interesting responses, ranging from pension schemes and engagement surveys to employee-of-the-month schemes.

It's often a similar story when talking about employer branding. As argued in Chapter 1, the terminology around employer branding is still being debated and defined. In a way, that is quite encouraging when working in a global context, because it allows you to actually ask the question 'What do we mean by employer branding?'

> *The discussion we have in our firm right now [is] the definition. What is the difference between employer branding and traditional branding? Is there a difference? And if so, what is the difference? This is interesting … The brand has to flow through the organisation, and all the staff members are a part of the brand. It is not only a project but also general changes in behaviour.*[1]

---

1   Peter Hemmingsen, HR manager, Ericsson, Denmark, Bernard Hodes Group, *Global Employer Brand Survey 2006*, p. 42.

Hodes US and UK conducted the *Hodes Global Network Survey* in 2006. This confirmed that some organisations, both clients and non-clients, still considered employer branding to be a pure recruitment tool. However, others had gone a step further and recognised that the need to deliver on the promises made by their recruitment communications was just as important and couldn't be ignored (see Figure 4.1).

A Purpose to Global Employer Branding

It was difficult to know whether to make this rule number one or rule number two on our list of 'golden rules'. They are equally important! And whilst some would say that this 'key to successfully delivering on a global stage is giving global employer branding a purpose' is a statement of the blindingly obvious, it is surprising that organizations do not give enough time to really defining this – particularly short term versus longer term. On the one hand, this is understandable given the pressure for immediate returns that so many organisations face today, but it is still a concern given that this is a journey and tangible results are measured in years, not months.

Given that growth is often the key business driver, attracting employees is often considered an immediate goal. It's easy to understand the thinking behind this, but, given the arguments advanced throughout this book, this goal should carry a large health warning – around establishing a global recruitment brand rather than an overarching global employer brand. In our view, it is a mistake to focus only on what you can promise as a global employer rather than on what you could actually deliver as a global employer.

In our experience, those that have avoided the trap have learnt from the initial insight phase. They've asked themselves what they need to do and how they need to change to present a more balanced and engaging global deal to their people. If we look to our colleagues in consumer marketing, the purpose of global branding is rarely, if ever, to achieve a 'one size fits all' solution. Yes, they want a brand to have a mark of consistency and promise but, at the same time, marketers want a brand to address the local needs of audiences, too. McDonalds is a good example. Its brand experience is the same throughout the world. However, as well as offering 'core' products like the Big Mac, it also serves traditional toasts and salad in France and pasta dishes in Italy – localising its offering for customers.

The most frequent employer branding expectations mentioned were: ease in attracting candidates (84 per cent), recognition as an employer of choice (82 per cent), increased retention rate (65 per cent), shortened time-to-fill (53 per cent) and delivery of a vision and values programme (52 per cent).

In the United Kingdom, the most frequently cited employer brand expectations also included higher job acceptance rate (65 per cent), setting a standard and framework for all human resources activity (62 per cent) and benefits to the service delivered to commercial customers (65 per cent).

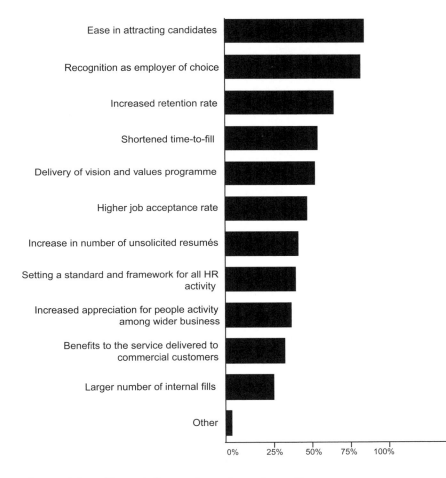

Figure 4.1   Expectations of employer branding

So why is that relevant to the present debate? Because it will help you understand how to position and plan the work on the Global Employer Brand. Unifying the organisation's global culture is rarely the aspiration in our experience, and it's a tall ambition if it were. More typically, it's about an aspect of the deal which will offer the individual a line of sight to the organisational purpose and deliver something in return, wherever they sit geographically in the organisation.

One of the most common aspects of the deal that global organisations will have to spend time considering is what opportunities 'being global' will bring them in terms of developing and managing their employer brand. Do aspects of the deal mean that employees can aspire to, and be rewarded by, the chance to travel with the organisation? Now, this is great if the business can deliver, but dangerous if there is no substance behind the promise. There's a world of difference between a shared global purpose and the universal question 'What's in it for me?'.

In a recent project with a large and successful global fast-moving consumer goods (FMCG) organisation, our discovery phase unveiled that the company still believed that it had a reputation for strong development and career opportunities. But, although this had been true in the past, research showed that it was no longer the case. Therefore, claiming that development was at the heart of its global deal would give talent joining the company false expectations. What's more, it would be questioned by existing employees and jeopardise their engagement.

For some organisations, the driver to give their employer brand stronger global appeal is to get talent to travel to them. For example, for some time organisations such as Transport for London have had to consider competing for engineering talent on an international, if not global, stage. If I am a Polish engineer, this is not about me joining Transport for London to travel the world. It's about Transport for London convincing me that it is worth moving from my home country to further my career. Another example is Saudi Aramco and its drive to persuade experienced Western petroleum engineers to move to the Saudi oil industry.

The Impact of 'Parent Culture'

Every culture has its starting-point – often the preferences of its founders and/or leaders. This is perfectly natural and, given the patterns of global trade which went unchallenged for centuries, it is hardly surprising that as the multinational emerged in recent decades, it was often dominated by the culture of its founding fathers.

Only in the 1990s did questions begin to arise as to whether this really was the best way to establish sustainable and ultimately successful operations beyond the founding territory. Organisations like M&S had bad experiences trying to expand into France and the US, and, equally famously, Disney hit some major issues when it tried to transport its 'theme park' formula to Europe.

Fons Trompenaars and Charles Hampden-Turner,[2] amongst others, have given us insight into national cultural behaviours, which helps to navigate in a world that is no longer 'getting' smaller, but is already smaller than ever before. Naturally, the more we know about local preferences, perceptions and engagement drivers of a given national culture, the easier it will be to understand how to build employer brands that are attractive and engaging. However, we must also take account of the parent culture because so often this dominates the management style within the organisation – and, as we have already said, people join brands and leave managers!

When talking about cultural differences and how to overcome them, people are typically looking for answers to questions like 'how best to deal with the Americans?' And most textbooks about national cultural awareness teach us about being sensitive to cultural norms in the mode of 'when in Rome, do as the Romans' – in other words, comply with local cultural behavioural preferences.

However, the aim should not be to just conform; it should be to constantly explore and find new ways of doing things for the better of the company, its customers and employees. Fruitful collaboration across borders is rooted in a deep belief that nobody (no culture) can claim to have the 'right' way of doing things, that everybody brings something to the table and that there isn't any right or wrong, just different ways of working. Local buy in and engagement is key in the global world. Due to the sheer size of most multicultural organisations, it is virtually impossible to be everywhere at anytime, let alone have any chance of knowing what is going on.

Too often, unfortunately, we are blinded by our own culture and 'common sense' – which can always only be 'common' to that culture' – and fail to understand that not every solution will travel over borders.

When working on the rebranding of France Telecom's mobile subsidiaries, the project team adopted the mantra: 'We are not here to disregard everything you, as a company, have done and achieved over the years with your local brand. We are here to build on your success and hopefully take the aspirations

---

2   Fons Trompenaars and Charles Hampden-Turner, *Riding the Waves of Culture*, Nicholas Brealey Publishing, London, 1997.

of the company even further.' Whilst this stimulated some good discussions in most Western European companies, the team had push back in one particular Eastern European company which viewed this mantra as an expression of stealing all its glory. Instead of taking the statement as a celebration and recognition of its past achievements, the company saw it as degrading.

It's worth remembering this when embarking on a global employer brand journey because, as previously argued, you never start from a blank piece of paper. As anyone who has worked with organisational culture development long before the world started talking about branding knows, it's not about whether you want an employer brand, it's about whether you want to manage it.

When defining your global brand the best audience to ask about reality and aspiration is your current employees. If your global considerations are kick-started as part of an M&A, then you have access to a vast cross-section of different audiences who will have an opinion about you, which it makes sense to investigate.

Clearly, it makes sense for organisations to clarify their situation when discussing the purpose of the global employer brand, and, we believe there are five possible scenarios to be in:

1.   natural growth – when an organisation chooses to set itself up in a new market from scratch;

2.   when an organisation needs to look outside its country of operation for scarce talent;

3.   two organisations coming together under a completely new brand (albeit one that may be a combination of both previous brands) – for example, Glaxo Welcome and SmithKline Beecham merging to become GSK in 2000;

4.   one organisation acquiring another organisation – the second organisation continues to operate under its existing brand, but has a fresh brand at parent level, an example being France Telecom's acquisition of Orange;

5.   one organisation subsuming/acquiring/merging with another organisation and losing its former brand to operate under the brand of the acquirer/dominant partner almost immediately – for example, RHM being acquired and merging into Premier Foods.

In all these likely scenarios the decision about the 'parent brand' will drive the positioning of the employer brand. In cultures dominated by an 'ascribed' status (versus achieved status)[3] there can be a tendency not to ask challenging questions about the perceptions of the parent brand. We would argue that it's a huge missed opportunity not to gain insight into your current positioning from an audience who would be pivotal to the building of a global employer brand. This is an ideal opportunity for them to share their viewpoints. But it is important to bear in mind that their perception of the employer brand will be influenced by: first, which of the above scenarios is in play; second, which 'side' they are speaking from; and, third, how they felt about the employer brand prior to any changes.

Balancing Global and Local

Fons Trompenaars summed up the challenge as the balance between consistency and adaptation that is needed for corporate success.[4] We have already alluded to this point but, rather than seeing this purely in a cultural context, we need to view it more in terms of the psychological contract and the practicality of organisational objectives.

In Chapter 3 we commented that the development of the psychological contract over the years was becoming more ideological. In global settings it's important to understand where the countries in question are on their journey. Could it be that the movement in the psychological contract is mainly relevant to the developed countries and that the less developed countries are potentially only on the verge of the relationship-based contract?

Our research activities worldwide suggest that key engagement drivers for similar roles in differing territories aren't necessarily the same. Although models like Maslow's Hierarchy of Needs[5] and, more recently, the work done by the Concours Institute and Age Wave[6] attempt to categorise the role of work in people's lives, what is an acceptable balance of risk and reward in one geography may well not be an acceptable balance in another.

---

3   Ibid.
4   Ibid., 'Chapter 1: 'An Introduction to Culture'.
5   A.H. Maslow, *Motivation and Personality* (2nd edn) Harper, New York, 1970.
6   Tamara J. Erickson and Lynda Gratton, 'A Job by Any Other Name' in 'What it Means to Work Here', *Harvard Business Review*, 85 (March 2007) pp. 104–112.

It reminds me of a story we were told as part of a cultural training programme. Two Western companies had pitched to win the contract to deliver a luggage-handling system to an airport in a small Asian country. The company that won the contract was the one that understood that, in this part of the world, cost efficiency was only half the story. Providing as much work as possible for the local community was the primary concern and that meant not reducing the number of employees who ran the machines. Another example is one faced by many global and local companies in parts of Africa: namely, their retention issues are not about their employees leaving to go and work for the competitors; rather, the main reason for losing employees is far more serious and that is death from AIDS.

We will talk more about global companies' social conscience in the final chapter and explore how companies are trying to adapt to a world where the different needs of a diverse workforce call for different actions.

The key to a successful employer brand is that the day-to-day experience of the organisation and its culture delivers on the promises made by the brand's position. In other words, the focus is on the way the business behaves in all the touchpoints throughout the employee lifecycle. Whilst we can agree that national culture has a strong impact on how well different ways of working go down in local settings, it's interesting to see how behavioural and motivational psychometric theories suggest that some ways of working could in fact be globally attractive.

The MBTI (Myers-Briggs Type Indicator)[7] argues that human behaviour can be explained by how we understand and make judgements about the world around us. The idea is that everyone has a certain set of preferences about how to do things and, arguably, these aren't restricted by national cultures. In fact, you could argue that individuals from very different national cultures could still have the same overall preference and therefore be the same type. The difference lies in the social and national context in which you have been

7   See http://www.myersbriggs.org/my-mbti-personality-type/mbti-basis. The purpose of
     Myers-Briggs Type Indicator personality inventory is to make the theory of psychological
     types described by C.G. Jung understandable and useful in people's lives. The essence of the
     theory is that much seemingly random behavioural variation is actually quite orderly and
     consistent, being due to basic differences in the ways individuals prefer to use their perception
     and judgement. 'Perception involves all the ways of becoming aware of things, people,
     happenings, or ideas. Judgment involves all the ways of coming to conclusions about what has
     been perceived. If people differ systematically in what they perceive and in how they reach
     conclusions, then it is only reasonable for them to differ correspondingly in their interests,
     reactions, values, motivations, and skills.'

bought up, and that some cultures might favour one preference over another, which is then seen as socially acceptable behaviour.

This is interesting if we remember the three different aspects of employee touchpoints: look and feel, tone of voice and behaviours. In this context, we can see that this opens up the opportunity to build policies, programmes and ways of working that could be globally engaging, despite potentially being seen as going against traditional cultural norms.

Orange articulated this very skilfully when working on rebranding France Telecom subsidiaries. Its focus was not to develop Orange in Romania, Orange in the Netherlands and Orange in Botswana, but in developing Orange Romania, Orange the Netherlands and Orange Botswana. This might just be seen as semantic, but in fact it's hugely significant. For the practitioner and the organisations whose employer brand they are developing, this cultural sensitivity is priceless and might potentially make the difference between a global proposition becoming a success or failure.

Conclusion

We are not going to pretend it's easy to develop and embed employer brands in a global setting. But we can promise is that it's a highly challenging and never boring piece of work.

Going global with your employer brand is likely to put you in the eye of the storm of organisational politics and expose you to agendas and debates that have been avoided or – even more challenging – actively discouraged. There may well be sensitivity around whether the heritage or name of the organisation is helping or hindering the global war for talent and engagement levels. Don't let preconceptions about the strength of the employer brand remain unchallenged. Going global is the time to tackle the perceptions and address the hidden and not-so-hidden agendas.

Never forget to ask the organisation to do its homework. What is your starting-point – natural growth or a M&A situation? The answer to this question will help you scope and plan how best to go about the development and not to do it all at once. Developing a global employer brand is in every way the famous elephant in the room, and it doesn't make sense to try to deal with it in one go. Be clear about the business case and purpose of your global employer brand. Use research to identify your current strengths and weaknesses. And plan your journey carefully, pinpointing your goals, deciding your priorities and picking which battles you fight and which you sidestep.

Last but not least, the biggest lesson we have learnt is about the value of global employer brands. Our experience suggests that such brands add maximum organisational value if they are developed and embedded in conjunction with the master brand positioning and applied to all the touchpoints of the employees' lifecycle in a way that is applicable to local cultures. We can't always promise an easy journey, but it will definitely be an eventful one!

PART II

THE DEAL IN PRACTICE

5

Sense and Simplicity – Uniting the Employee and Customer Proposition

Jo Pieters
Vice President Global Recruitment, Philips International

Job Mensink
Senior Director Recruitment Marketing, Philips International

Until a few years ago, each Philips business or site took responsibility for communicating with their separate talent markets. There was no single message that would give candidates an idea what it would be like to work with us or what our culture was about. The result was a scattered approach that sent different messages, made different promises and offered different benefits. Of course, some of these messages were quite appealing and effective, but there was no real consistency. This situation made it very difficult for Philips to establish and build effective links with talented people at universities and business schools. The problem was even more pronounced when it came to attracting top talent interested in international careers.

Brands exist in the hearts and minds of people. They have the power to captivate, interest and communicate. We wanted and needed to create a space where we could define our brand promise and values. What's more, we wanted to ensure that the brand we created appealed to every segment of our talent market.

All companies look for talent, or at least claim they're looking for talent. Just getting people's attention by differentiating your organisation from all the others can be a huge challenge in itself.

Marketing gurus tell us that in order to stand out, you have to stand for something. The 'value proposition' should be the most compelling reason or feeling that will make talented candidates decide to join a company. To engage and motivate, the proposition has to be unique and attractive. But it doesn't end there. To create value for both the company and the candidate there has to be a strong and sustainable match of supply and demand. This can only work if the proposition is true and accurate. After all, it's not just about signing a contract. Empty or false promises will not lead to engaged and productive colleagues. Promoting a company as an employer of choice isn't just about creating a nice image. It's about attracting and engaging people with a story that is appealing, unique and, above all, true.

When we investigated how people develop their attitudes toward potential employers, it became clear that we could compare the process to certain aspects of consumer buying behaviour. When a candidate considers joining a company, the decision-making process is analogous to a purchasing decision. In fact, people go through specific 'pre-sales' and 'sales' phases. The first phase is very much about orientation and information, and people create a (more or less articulated) shortlist of companies they would like to consider. The second phase is more interactive and includes conversations and interviews with the companies that appear on the list.

Along the way, we can define a series of 'touchpoints'. Each one of these is a moment of truth that has to reflect the company's proposition to the candidate (see Figure 5.1). A touchpoint is an instance when people interact with a brand. Each of these occasions is an opportunity to strengthen or weaken your brand. They are an essential tool for understanding exactly why people make the choices that they do.

For example, if the career website presents the company as caring and supportive and you are interviewed by someone who is dominant and unfeeling, the company loses credibility. In the end, people will only select a company that presents itself consistently and authentically in all interactions. Whilst candidates don't buy jobs, they certainly buy into companies.

We saw touchpoints as an opportunity to define the design principles we needed to develop a global approach to recruitment marketing. We knew exactly where we needed to start – with our own employees. By talking to them we could find out what it's really like to work with Philips.

Touchpoints: the 'moments of truth' that attract and engage talented people	
Before joining	• Advertising & PR • Job fairs • Website • Internships • Business challenge • Interviews ...
After joining	• On-boarding programmes • Management style • Learning programmes • Referral programmes • Online community • Alumni networks ...

Figure 5.1   Touchpoints: the moments of truth

Straight from the Horse's Mouth

Our first step was to create a multidisciplinary project team that included people from our core business and the regions, as well as external research experts and communication specialists. We borrowed this model from our innovation teams in product marketing, and it proved very valuable. To reach deeper insights and breakthrough ideas, it's essential to try to step outside your normal patterns of thinking. This has proven to work best in new groups made up of people from different business areas. Different backgrounds, beliefs and approaches can result in unique and compelling insights.

Diversity should be an important feature of any company, and perhaps even more so in a multinational organisation. To deliver on our brand promise to customers, we had to be as diverse as our customers are. To this end, we had to focus on gender and cultural, as well as geographical, diversity. We needed to have an approach that was relevant and inclusive for all the different backgrounds we found among our current employees and our potential talent pool.

Then we organised focus group discussions and one-to-one interviews around the world to develop insights and big ideas around 'working for Philips'. Valuable information was also generated by the general employee engagement survey. More than 90,000 people take part in this every year. These findings were put together and tested in dedicated surveys that included more than 10,000 colleagues.

Talking Frankly to Candidates – and Competitors

After getting initial results and ideas from the internal survey, we looked towards the world outside Philips in order to find out what talented candidates thought of us. At the same time, we needed to discover what best practice meant to other companies. For the candidate perspective, we used available market research as well as dedicated interviews and surveys. Important insights also came from interviewing 'lost candidates' who had decided not to take our job offers, as well as from 'regretted losses' or exit interviews with people who had decided to leave of their own accord. Using Philips' marketing tools for consumer insights and value propositions gave us a clear structure to plan our research, unite our data and arrive at a small set of 'big ideas' for our overall proposition.

Finding a Global Employee Value Proposition

When you start looking for reasons why people sign with a company and why they decide to stay, you encounter a wide range of ideas and impressions. We identified many of these in the qualitative interview rounds. However, the only way to test these as propositions was to validate them both internally and externally. What we were looking for was one overall promise underpinned by a number of 'reasons-to-believe' (see Figure 5.2).

The biggest challenge for the overall proposition is ensuring that it makes the grade with two 'customers': the company and the prospective candidates. Full endorsement from the company leadership is essential; without this, it's impossible to implement the new brand in any consistent way. Second – and this will be a key question for the company – you must be able to verify that the proposition is indeed attractive, unique and credible to talented people who are not currently employed by the business.

MAKING RELATIONSHIPS COUNT

At the core of all our plans for progress is the relationship that begins with a candidate and continues when that person becomes an employee. We've

1. Target/Player	2. Candidate Insights	3. Competitive Environment
Who are we looking for? What are their interests, values and attitudes?	Which candidate need/dilemma or problem are we addressing? What do they really want?	Which alternative organisations are the candidates considering? How are they perceived?

4. Benefit for Target	5. Reasons to Believe	6. Discriminator
What is the emotional and functional benefit for the candidate to join Philips?	Which 3–5 concrete aspects of working at Philips illustrate the benefits and make them credible?	The single-minded, most compelling factor that will make talented candidates decide to want to join Philips.

Brand Pillars

Royal Philips Electronics 2008 ©

Figure 5.2   The employee value proposition house
© Royal Philips Electronics 2008.

identified four separate stages. The aim of each new stage is to make it easy for people to continue to the next step. Each phase has its own challenges and opportunities. Different types of communication are more effective in one phase than in another. Figure 5.3 offers a closer look at the four stages.

This approach makes it possible to establish the company's strengths and weaknesses across different regional markets and talent segments. The operational plan and budget for any market should be based on an assessment of the health of the employer brand in each of the phases, followed by priority- and objective-setting. This level of assessment is essential to any future planning and development.

CONSISTENCY THROUGH TOUCHPOINTS

Once the overall proposition was agreed internally and validated externally, the real work could begin. Now we were confident that we could use our findings across all markets and touchpoints. At this stage, we had to make sure that the brand was brought to life in all our brochures, websites, events and even our interviews. With this in mind, we agreed an approach that outlined respective roles and responsibilities for the global team as well as for the country teams. In principle, we wanted all brand development to be completed centrally, and most of the brand activation brought to life locally, using a toolkit of materials that

Four stages	Dominant Marketing Principle	Typical marketing instruments
1.Consideration *Creating the interest to actively consider opportunities at the company.*	**One to Many** The company broadcasts to the whole world *=> becoming less effective*	• Advertising • Free publicity • Job fairs
2. Commitment *Presenting relevant opportunities and creating the commitment to join.*	**One to Few** Communicate with selected target groups	• Website • Internships • Interviews
3. Contribute *Providing an engaging environment for personal growth and contribution.*	**One to One** Driven mostly by the manager, personal contact	• On-boarding programmes • Management style • Learning programmes
4. Commending *Making it easy for people to share their enthusiasm for Philips as an employer with others.*	**Many to Many** Not the company but employees communicate in different networks *=> becoming more effective*	• Referral programmes • Online community • Alumni networks

Figure 5.3　　Four stages in the talent–company relationship

could be translated or adapted as needed. Identity guidelines would also be on hand to help us all to achieve consistency. An important factor in all of this was the global team. It was not a team that actually worked at our headquarters, but a virtual team that included our key country recruitment marketing managers. The global agenda and key initiatives were agreed, or at least endorsed, by the countries before work actually began.

IMPACT

The change from a local-for-local to a global-and-local approach worked very well for our positioning across the different talent markets. Figure 5.4 illustrates our improvements in recruiting technical and commercial talent across key markets.

We discovered that our communications were more visible, better appreciated and more effective in driving people to events or to our website. Primarily this was because they now resonated with our corporate and product advertising. Having the same look and feel makes it easy for people to recognise Philips more quickly and direct their attention towards career opportunities.

Before we took a more global approach, the look and feel of our recruitment marketing communications was designed by small agencies or HR managers.

Europe – Ranking of Philips

Engineering & Science	2003	2004	2005	2006
Familiar with Philips (rank)	24	14	9	7
Considered employer	6	5	3	4
Ideal employer	#21	#17	#17	#12
Business	2003	2004	2005	2006
Familiar with Philips (rank)	25	21	12	13
Considered employer	16	11	8	8
Ideal employer	#65	#62	#54	#51

Europe – Ranking of Philips
(target universities)

Engineering & Science	2003	2004	2005	2006
Familiar with Philips	17	11	9	6
Considered employer	15	9	6	4
Ideal employer	#14	#8	#4	#4
Business	2003	2004	2005	2006
Familiar with Philips	26	17	11	9
Considered employer	23	11	8	4
Ideal employer	#20	#9	#5	#5

Figure 5.4   Improving our position

Very often, the people involved were enthusiastic and determined to make their own mark, but not necessarily looking for the best way to leverage our established marketing communications. When we take into account the investment levels for the recruitment market versus consumer advertising, it comes down to a ratio that's on the order of 1:100. So, there's a clear and coherent argument for leveraging what we see as an impressive asset. After the launch of the Sense and Simplicity campaign, we continued to build on our shared identity.

Our initiative also had an important internal effect. Using a more structured approach to recruitment marketing as a starting-point, we established an international professional network. They exchanged best practice, shared materials and ideas with each other and met regularly at international team events.

We also connected people by building new networks that accelerated their development and created new roles that were much more rewarding and fulfilling than their previous ones. There were also new positions in the HR structure, both global and nationally, that facilitated cross-functional people development. These roles could be filled by people moving from Marketing to HR or vice versa. For us, this represented a unique way of moving talented people into new, and even interdisciplinary, roles.

In addition to all the internal and external changes that our branding work brought about (see Figure 5.5), we also received plenty of professional recognition, including awards.

Change is Ongoing

Looking at the results of our market research and Figure 5.2 in particular, we can make some important observations. While we have put our house in order and achieved significant improvements compared to five years ago, we're by no means at the end of our efforts.

Our progress has definitely been exciting, but at a certain point it also started flattening out. This could be the result of increasingly tight talent markets, or even down to our competitors developing their own initiatives. What's more, our position in the market reflects our traditional talent needs, not what our current needs are. But we're certainly not the only business in this situation. Many companies will recognise most, if not all, of these concerns.

LETTING NUMBERS SPEAK FOR THEMSELVES

In consumer brand management, it's common practice to measure the 'state of the brand' using three key metrics that reflect awareness, consideration and preference. The underlying logic is that, to be successful, you need to pass through a few very well-defined hoops. Until people are aware of, or familiar with, your brand you will not be able to establish an ongoing relationship with them.

Specific marketing instruments are available to improve the performance of a brand in these metrics. Mass media advertising will help to raise awareness, but it is almost impossible to improve preference with advertising alone. People's hearts and minds can only really be won when they have a fulfilling experience with the product or services. This means that once a certain level

before 2004
confusion is not convincing

after 2005
more effective and efficient

Figure 5.5   Old and new communications

of consideration is achieved, it is more effective and efficient to shift mass media investments towards more engaging and personal communication paths. Alongside changes in the market, our next phase would see us find different ways of communicating and building relationships with potential candidates.

TIGHTER TALENT MARKETS

In all of our markets, we're finding it increasingly difficult to attract qualified candidates. One of the drivers behind this is economic growth. Another important factor is the relative mismatch between what people choose to study and what companies would like to hire. As a result, we see a shortage in a number of technology and IT areas across different markets. A third and more fundamental concern for Western markets is simply a demographic trend. Baby-boomers are beginning to retire at a higher rate than graduates are entering the market, and the workforce as a whole is contracting. This means that the 'battle for talent' will only become more intense.

THE COMPETITION HEATS UP

Now, many companies are putting more energy and resources into their recruitment marketing activities. This is easily demonstrated by the increased levels of media investment across the entire recruitment marketing arena, including everything from new websites to graduate events and fully integrated campaigns. For example, in the Netherlands alone we saw an increase in spending of more than 40 per cent in 2006–2007 across the sector. It's a trend that we can see at every level, from local to global.

TRADITIONAL VERSUS NEW

As a consequence of our business strategy, the Simplicity promise and the focus on healthcare, lifestyle and lighting, we are now moving from a technology-driven company to one that's driven by end-users. This change requires more outside-in thinking, market focus and entrepreneurial behaviour than before. It demands creativity and bright ideas that aren't just the result of technical research. And that means we need to attract and include people with different talents. Today, in every talent market our position is stronger in the technology segments than in business areas. It's now clear that we need to find new and better ways to address this candidate group.

The Second Wave – It's All about Love

Everything we learned helped us prepare for the next phase of our development. As a first step, we set up a series of qualitative interviews with graduates and experienced MBA students. From this research, we found that people today are more demanding than we expected. Not only are they focused on the job and potential career prospects, but they're also concerned about future colleagues, the working environment and the larger social purpose and role of the organisation.

Next, we exchanged ideas with some great companies like Starbucks, Nike and Google. What they all have in common is an incredibly clear focus on delivering a great customer experience. But there's more. They have also been able to establish a culture that celebrates and develops the competencies and practices that will improve the customer experience.

We found that these companies develop and actively nurture the connection between a very happy customer ('I love what I get') and that of a highly engaged worker ('I love what I do'). This insight brings Marketing and HR together in an entirely new and potentially powerful way. This is about selecting and developing people in terms of their enthusiasm, energy and competencies for doing what is needed to create the best customer experience. It's about celebrating our own products, our pride in them and our knowledge of them. The goal is to focus an entire organisation not only on doing things in a way its people really love, but also on delivering solutions that customers love.

This whole idea represents a genuine change in our thinking. Young people have become more demanding and are looking for more than just opportunities to accelerate their own careers. A company based on a big idea, an authentic identity, creates a certain appeal – one that you can either like or dislike. This means that an organisation attracts people from a position of strength – one that can't be reached by using a mainstream or more generally appealing idea. As in human relationships, the opposite of love is indifference, not hate. So a company in search of a passionate relationship with a defined group of employees will have to 'unattract' a group.

ALIGNMENT WITH SIMPLICITY

The connection we describe helps a company to drive energy and engagement from employees directly to customers. Two common elements appear to be fully embedded in the culture of each of the companies we got closer to. First is a range of activities that can be described as 'brand rituals'. Second, the firm's products are extensively used and enjoyed among its employees, as shown in Figure 5.6. An example of such rituals is the coffee-tasting that takes place at the opening of Starbucks' meetings. Different blends are tasted and, as people talk about their preferences, they develop their own taste and vocabulary for the coffee experience that they will later offer their customers. People in office roles also participate, so the experience isn't limited only to customer-facing staff. For the same reason, employees also get a free pack of coffee every week So that they can enjoy the coffee experience in their homes, too.

Translating this idea into the Philips simplicity promise has resulted in a number of initiatives aimed at both candidates and employees. What we want to achieve is a candidate experience that brings simplicity to life (see Table 5.1).

New Ways to Connect with Talent

The value of communication is determined by feedback. Content is obviously key, but so is the medium that we choose. Traditional media including, for example, print advertising now generates fewer and fewer responses. People increasingly prefer video over pictures and listening over reading.

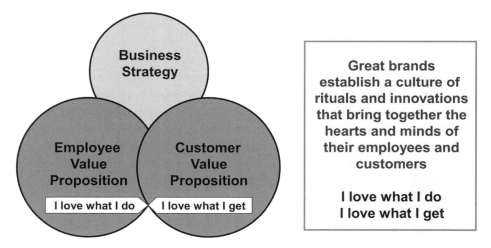

Figure 5.6   **Circles of love: linking employees to the customer proposition**

Table 5.1   'Brand rituals' inspire employees to serve their customers
             better

Brand rituals	Celebrating own products
Examples from observed companies Coffee-tasting at the start of international meetings Using excellent sporting facilities during workdays **Philips examples** Simplicity Day: Worldwide event to develop ideas to improve and simplify ways of working Testing all new products in experience centres and celebrating results (or corrective actions) Improving and developing new ideas on simplicity: Is the idea based on insights, is it providing exciting new benefits, is it really easy to use?	**Examples from observed companies** Getting a free pack of coffee every week Staff shop with new products every two weeks culture of only using own products **Philips examples** 'Ambassador' programmes offering new products at very low prices Using Philips products as gifts instead of gift cheques Making products and advertising materials more visible in the 'formerly' sparce offices

Above all, people like to get the inside story directly from others. Our qualitative research with graduates demonstrated the powerful impact that internships can have on opinions of future employers. This applies not only to the student participating in the internship, but to that intern's entire class.

We decided that the best way to address this insight was to put in place new initiatives aimed at connecting with future talent. And that's exactly what we did. Now we offer more structured internship programmes that help us identify candidates and create positive experiences that students naturally want to share. We've also created interactive video portraits for our website that focus on honest communications and provide insights into people's work, colleagues, environments and development (see Figure 5.7). We're attracting people to Philips by creating relationships. For us, it's about consistent messages and finding new and better ways to deliver them.

Lessons Learned

In the long run, the only way to achieve success is to attract talented people who become passionate ambassadors for your business and

Figure 5.7   The inside story: interactive video portraits

what it stands for. It's not about inventing a nice image and selling this to potential employees. You have to be able to convey the unique and attractive characteristics of your company in an honest and open way. This process has to start inside the organisation. In fact, we think that only by looking deeply into your organisation can you capture key values and characteristics. A good starting-point is employee engagement or satisfaction surveys. They can offer a good initial overview of perceived strengths and weaknesses. A next step could be an interviewing phase in which you find out what it is really like to work for your company, what your colleagues think is great and, of course, what they think isn't so great.

You should also take a look at frustrations or weaknesses. Not only do you want to understand today's strengths, you also need to stay focused on the future. One of the tools that can direct this research is the development and testing of employee insights. An insight describes a person (target) in a certain situation, with a problem or dilemma and a desired result. This insight can be brought into focus groups or one-to-one interviews for further development. Selecting the strongest insight means testing it to see if it has certain qualities such as a unique appeal for candidates, resonance with current employees and a solid fit with the company strategy. Any resulting proposition can be validated by rigorous online testing across all relevant markets.

LOVE

Your positioning should start with the strongest insight that also fits in with the larger company strategy. What you need to find is the link that takes you from the 'I love what I do' for employees to the 'I love what I get' from customers. What captures the very essence of the company? There is no easy way to find this lynch pin. You need a deep understanding of the customer brand promise and knowledge of the core competences, values and practices that make it possible to deliver on the brand promise (see Figure 5.8).

There are four critical phases in the talent–company relationship (the 4-C framework):

1.   *Consider*. Candidates go from being unaware to *considering*, which means actively trying to find out more about a company – 'I want to know more'.

2.   *Commit*. Candidates get more information and discover more, finding the company so attractive and distinctive that they want to *commit* and apply for a role.

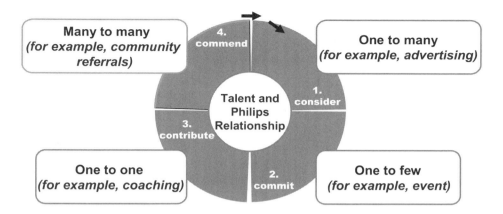

Figure 5.8   The 4-C recruitment marketing framework in action

3.   *Contribute.* After they are hired, candidates are engaged and developed so that they *contribute* to the company mission.

4.   *Commend.* Engaged employees turn into 'net promoters' or ambassadors who *commend* the company to others.

The purpose of employer branding is to make it easy and appealing for candidates to move on to the next phase. The framework in Figure 5.8 illustrates how each phase has its own communication characteristics that you need to manage as employer brand manager:

•   *Phase 1 – Consider.* You don't yet know the prospective candidate. You need to use *one-to-many* communications like broadcasting — however this becomes less and less effective.

•   *Phase 2 – Commit.* Candidates have come forward, and you can target segments more effectively – *one-to-few* communications already have more impact.

•   *Phase 3 – Contribute.* Here, it's the manager who is the most important 'brand deliverer', so *one-to-one* communications have very high impact (although it is already more difficult to manage the managers).

•   *Phase 4 – Commend.* Here is the new marketing reality. The company is no longer alone in the driving seat – people connect to people and it is *very* difficult to drive *many-to-many* communications. The only way to manage them is to have engaged, passionate employees, which means you have to be honest and authentic.

If you play this right, fewer less effective *one-to-many* communications are needed because word-of-mouth takes over.

Perhaps telling two stories makes it complicated, but it is interesting how four generations of marketing principles, which started with broadcasting (one-to-many) and is now social network marketing (*many-to-many*) are totally relevant for how to look at the talent-company relationship.

THE WHOLE FUNNEL

After you've collected insights and defined your positioning, you can start to bring all this to life through the four stages of the employer relationship. You might inaugurate this phase by extending the existing research to diagnose your performance in each of the phases, relative to that of key competitors. Depending on the levels of employer brand awareness, consideration and preference, you can determine which areas need attention and action. On an international level, this kind of analysis can help you determine how a budget can be best allocated across different markets and where highest returns can be expected.

At Philips we've been able to start measuring just how successful uniting the employer and customer proposition can be. It was an amazing undertaking, and one that's still with us today. And we will continue building on what we've learned well into the future.

6

From Poor M&S to Your M&S – The Historical Perspective

Keith Cameron
Human Resources Director, Marks & Spencer (2004–2008)

No employer brand is static. I believe that your reputation as an employer evolves and changes over time, and it's only really possible to understand the nature and strength of your employer proposition if you look at it historically.

As HR practitioners, I think it's very rare that we make the time to step back and look at what we're doing in a historical context. This is a great shame. There are huge lessons to be learned from corporate history – about the changing relationship between corporate and employer values, about what happens to the employer brand in moments of crisis, about the human condition, even. Look closely and you'll find all these facets in the M&S story.

The Age of the Great Machine

Speaking as M&S's unofficial corporate historian – and this really is my view and nobody else's – there are essentially three ages of M&S. The first of these ran from 1884 to 1998 – from the early foundation years to about a decade ago when the business began to falter.

I call this period the Age of the Great Machine. Commercial life was simpler, the competition was less sophisticated and the business was in the ascendant. Throughout these years, M&S was like a great golden, beautifully manufactured and perfectly oiled machine; one that knew nothing but success. It seemed to generate profits effortlessly and dominated the high street for generations.

If you examine this period, it's clear that a lot of our commercial success was formulaic. In some ways, that's hardly surprisingly. We led the market for so long and so successfully that it's only to be expected that we refined and perfected our processes and developed successful formulas and models for doing business. What made the formula more interesting was that it actually permitted a great deal of innovation.

Clearly, there's something of a paradox here. On the one hand, we were a very conservative and predictable business through the first 100 years or so of our history. We had a carefully modulated response to change, continuously readjusting the formula and planning out new courses of action to respond to new challenges. Yet, on the other hand, this templated and unspontaneous way of doing business generated some of the most far-reaching breakthroughs in retail.

Look back on this period and you can see we were at the forefront of a host of technical improvements – in both clothing and food. Lycra was developed and widely adopted as a material thanks to M&S, and we pioneered the notion of convenience foods and take-away sandwiches. Interestingly, though, all these developments were supported by the conservative, risk-averse approach we had at the time – we trialled and piloted all the innovations methodically, making sure that the technical and logistical case for any sort of change was completely watertight.

And, of course, this rigorously scientific approach to innovation was a great success. Now, two decades later, and with the benefit of hindsight, we can see that this success was actually a very mixed blessing. It fed the internal perception that the cautious, formulaic approach to change was the right response and, even more destructively, it began to instil a sense of arrogance in the business.

In simple terms, we began to lose touch with our customers. We became intoxicated with our commercial success and began to think it was a measure of how well attuned to our customers we were, rather than a reflection of how slowly our competitors reacted. We were in a benign market, but we never realised it – or we certainly never acknowledged it to ourselves.

Elsewhere, other retailers were waking up. In the late 1990s, I remember looking over the fence at M&S when I was at Arcadia and thinking, 'They must be very clever. They must know something we don't.' Everyone on the high street was buying space in out-of-town retail parks, except M&S – and it troubled us. Now we know that it needn't have. M&S's reluctance to move away from its prime pitches on the high streets was far from clever; rather, it was based on the misconception that its customers wouldn't want to alter their shopping habits for a new experience. How wrong it was. The company completely failed to understand the attraction of parking close to a store and then wheeling your buggy around a large single-storey building in relative comfort. Escalators are the devil's own devices if you're shopping with a pushchair and children in tow, but this fact seemed lost on the M&S management of old.

Similarly, our lack of changing rooms until recently reveals an alarming lack of commercial foresight and customer understanding. Not only did it frustrate customers, but it also led us to adopt an overgenerous returns policy. We refunded items without question for many weeks after they were purchased, partly as an indirect way of compensating people because there was nowhere to try anything on. Indeed, we became so well known for our generosity that there are a few legendary incidents of people returning items decades after they bought them – and M&S honouring the return. All very noble, but hardly the best way to sharpen performance.

PEOPLE IN THE AGE OF THE GREAT MACHINE

M&S was very paternalistic towards its people in this first stage of its development. That's not to say the relationship was ineffective; it clearly worked fairly well as sales and profits grew exponentially. But I do believe that the deal between employer and employee during what I call the Age of the Great Machine was a parent–child one. The management proclaimed, and employees listened.

When I joined M&S in 2004 I reviewed all our HR policies and processes and there are thousands of examples of this adult–child relationship. Let me share one. M&S's company car policy of old was an encyclopaedic tome. All in all, the policy ran to about 16 pages of small print, outlining what benefits and vehicles people were entitled to, what criteria they needed to fulfil and their responsibilities as company car owners. The highlight of the policy, from my perspective – the point that really underlined the paternalism in the organisation at that time – was a statement saying that after you have been driving for two hours you must take a 15-minute break. It's a wonderful indication of the place M&S occupied in many of its people's lives – part caring employer, part overcautious parent.

One of our biggest challenges has been to adjust this relationship and shift the balance from adult–child to adult–adult. It has not been easy. However, I think we're slowly getting there and can now give people a number of options and trust that they have the confidence and expertise to make an informed decision.

The Age of Uncertainty

For almost everyone in retail, 1998 was a memorable year, but for M&S it marked the beginning of a whole new era. The clothing market basically collapsed in that year. We all felt it. I was at Arcadia at the time, and trade for us – as for almost everyone else – simply fell off a cliff.

However, we did what many others retailers did. We put our heads down, pared everything to the bone, renegotiated everything we could, including our overseas manufacturing contracts, set in place a raft of tactical discounts and braced ourselves for a rough ride.

Across town, M&S's response was a little different: it froze. In simple terms, the Great Golden Machine couldn't cope; it wasn't configured for these sorts of conditions. Yes, of course, the management had experienced downturns before, but 1998 wasn't a 24-hour typhoon; it was the beginning of a Force 10 storm that was to play out over many years.

At M&S, senior management was spending a disproportionate amount of time on matters other than trading. Poor results meant that the leadership had to change. Succession politics took up far too much of the board's time. The new top team decided to try to reverse the paternalistic employee approach of the old order. They brought in an operating policy called 'Be Free', which was premised on individual initiative and autonomy and on taking responsibility for your own decisions. So, in a relatively short space of time, we went from clear corporate structure, top-down decision-making and a parent–child, employer–employee relationship to blurred lines of responsibility and a wealth of management initiatives.

In many ways, it was anarchic. There was a palpable lack of conviction behind many of the initiatives and programmes at the time. We increased our product range, but the result was more confusion, rather than more choice – we had 16 different versions of black trousers for women. What's more, there was a sense of rebellion on the shop floor, which was the result of the old overindulgent culture and a general feeling that the management didn't quite know what it was doing.

All this confusion filtered down to the bottom line; there were boardroom changes, and in 2003 our profits were under pressure as never before. This marks the nadir of the M&S story and ushers in Stuart Rose's appointment in 2004. It also represents the beginning of what I call the third and most recent era in M&S's development: the Age of Simplicity.

The Age of Simplicity

The beginning of this period and the interest from Philip Green has been well documented, so I don't want to repeat a familiar story. However, this was the point at which I joined the business, and I do think it's worth putting down my first impressions as it gives some indication of just how far we have come in three years or so.

Without doubt, there's an extraordinarily strong culture here. Because it has developed over so many years there's a definite sense of the M&S way. There's a network of influence which is initially quite hard to penetrate and there is a gentle quality to do with doing the best by people that pervades the whole business.

I also noticed very early on that the quality of people in M&S is very good, although they aren't always used to their full capacity. And, finally, the accent here is on thinking rather than doing. Planning and calculating is one of the things that the business does best, and, for some people, it's almost a default mode of behaviour.

In many ways, culturally M&S is reminiscent of the civil service. There's a fantastic sense of tradition, the place is full of bright people, but there is also this mandarin sense of detachment. Minimising risks and justifying decisions are as important as the action itself.

Add all these qualities together and it makes for quite a sense of inertia. When I joined I never experienced any great urgency, which is worrying. Retail is about speed – introducing a new line at a crucial time can make all the difference to profits; pioneering a new people practice can have an enormous impact on retention. However, that drive simply wasn't there three years ago. It is now.

RE-ESTABLISHING THE BRAND VALUES

The speed of progress we've made in the last three years is down to a range of factors, not least Stuart's understanding of the business. He began his career here and rose to senior management level before moving to the Burton Group, so he is very well attuned to the culture of the place. In particular, he was able to see the great equity that was still in the M&S values: Quality, Service, Value, Innovation and Trust.

He realised that, to transform the business, it wasn't necessary to rotate it 360°. Instead, he has concentrated on breathing life into, and delivering, our existing values and harnessing the strength of the qualities that the business was long known for.

The HR challenge, of course, has been to take these brand values and translate them into models for individual employee behaviour. As you would expect, this has involved an extensive change management programme, involving our people, our processes and our culture.

THE KEY STAGES OF CHANGE

In broad terms, our change programme went through three phases: Focus, Drive and Broaden.

The first phase was all about identifying the essentials and making sure that anything peripheral didn't use up a disproportionate amount of financial investment or time. For instance, we made sure from the outset that we were very disciplined with our capital expenditure – programmes were scaled back or halted.

Drive, as the name suggests, is to do with productivity and how quickly we could get the machine up and running. It's important to drive really hard early on, build some impetus and then keep that momentum going. We've worked hard to create that early pace because that was absent from the business we found in 2004, and long-term success depends on it.

The Broaden heading is about thinking beyond where we are now; about looking at new service lines and markets – even new territories. It's where we are today. We're now expanding internationally, increasing our product offering and developing our service lines, but only because the first two stages of the programme are in place.

PRODUCT, SERVICE, ENVIRONMENT

We began with very clear ends in sight. We set out to transform our product, our service and our environment; because by focusing on these three objectives we knew we could change the entire M&S landscape.

We're some distance along the road, although we're by no means there yet. In terms of product, we've simplified our ranges, introduced a raft of more contemporary lines and tightened up our commercial practices. Among other areas, we've radically rethought our buying function, and this has had a profound impact on our margins.

Until relatively recently, the buying function here was separated from the selecting function. Buyers were buyers in name only. They would select products, materials and ingredients from around the world, but that's where their role ended as they did not negotiate the cost price of any of their selections. So they would make a recommendation to head office which would then purchase the item. To call the system flawed is somewhat overgenerous. Materials would be selected on the basis of their style and quality, with insufficient thought about their cost or commercial competitiveness. And, the result, unsurprisingly, was that our margins suffered terribly.

We reversed this industry anomaly by reskilling buyers and merchandisers and redefining the terms of their role. This involved sending over 900 people to our specially designed buying academy.

Similarly, we're addressing the environment part of our offer with similar commitment. In this area we've had something of a head-start. We've inherited some very good design proposals, which have been enthusiastically greeted in the business. By the end of 2008 we will have rolled out a complete in-store refurbishment across our whole network within three years.

Improving the service element of what we do is perhaps the most complex challenge we face, and it's certainly the one that impacts on the people agenda most significantly.

When I first arrived in the business, service was in something of a crisis. Some sections of the shop floor were disillusioned, and this translated into very poor staff and management visibility. Back then it was a common customer criticism that people couldn't find a customer assistant when they needed one – they had a tendency to go missing or take shelter behind their clipboards.

There was this strange preconception among some staff and managers that serving customers was a lower priority than various other departmental tasks – stocktaking, refilling shelves and so on. There was a problem with product knowledge, although, paradoxically, product knowledge on the shop floor was very good. But there did seem to be a lack of confidence among customer-facing people; our staff were out of practice; they were not having enough interaction with our customers.

TAKING A LEAD ON TRAINING

Addressing this lack of confidence was one of our first people initiatives of the new era. We had to get 60,000 people up to speed in double-quick time. It actually took us just over a year – training groups of 5,000 at a time. We developed our service style together with Mary Gober, who has spent many years refining a confidence-based approach to customer service training. Part-evangelical sermon, part shock-tactic, the approach builds self-belief and gives people the resilience to handle customer issues. It was just what was needed.

MANAGING THE UNMANAGEABLE: PAY IN FOCUS

However, training was only one aspect of the story. Three years ago the rewards were also in urgent need of attention. I was very surprised when I arrived that the starting pay on the shop floor was only a few pence above the national minimum wage. M&S has this excellent reputation for its terms and conditions, but in terms of pay this had been eroded over time and we had to work quite hard to restore it. We're now the second-best payer on the high street after John Lewis – a position that reflects our resourcing strategy and commitment to hiring good people.

The problem with pay was compounded by having 56,000 customer assistants working to a single job description and being paid 429 different pay rates. We've gone through a huge restructuring process, which has included removing long-service pay, pushing back the pay review date by three months and abolishing a bonus scheme that was failing to motivate anyone. Our new structure is far simpler: as well as establishing four pay rates, we paid a one-off cash bonus to anyone whose rates didn't go up. In 2005 over 40 per cent of our customer assistants received a lump-sum payment rather than a rate increase.

One of our most successful initiatives was to introduce a new role to the shop floor: coach. We've some extremely knowledgeable and experienced customer-facing people, and this new role gave them the chance to maximise their abilities. What's more, it established a structured career path for people to follow, as the role sat at a higher level than a customer assistant and attracted higher rewards.

Previously, we would have debated and deliberated something as far-reaching as a mass role-creation scheme into oblivion. There would have been all sorts of questions about the optimum ratio of coaches to staff and the correct way to assess them. Then we would have referred the decision to a consultant to gain an objective perspective and, by the time we had paid their fees, we would have lost any of the commercial advantage it could have given us.

We took a rather different approach. We made the decision about the new role, then shortly after we asked for volunteers to train into it. In all, some 8,000 people came forward. And we ended up training all 8,000 of them in an intensive two-day programme. Another exercise in mass development and another great success.

A RELATIONSHIP BUILT ON RESPECT

As well as initiatives designed to grow our people, we also made a concerted effort to address poor performance. This has never been one of M&S's strengths. We've been overtolerant of poor performance – a legacy of our conservative, risk-averse approach to change.

In the past, we've overcomplicated the disciplinary procedure. However, we've now reduced the number of steps in the process from five to three, which means we're able to address issues quicker and much more effectively.

THE VIRTUOUS CIRCLE

The objective of this multi-strand approach to improving service is to create a virtuous circle (see Figure 6.1). We have begun to achieve a self-perpetuating round of training and development and of rewards and performance measures that generates higher service standards. We started by defining our expectation of good service for both trainees and qualified people and then putting in place the career structure, development and rewards that would enable people to

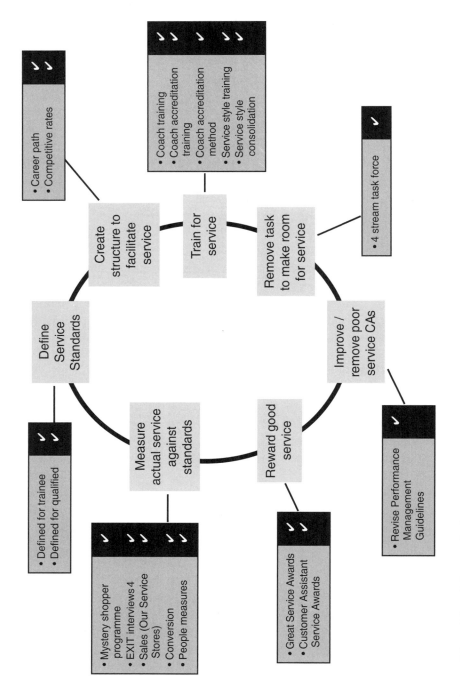

Figure 6.1   The virtuous circle

reach these standards. In effect, the points in the circle represent stages along the journey that we have made since 2004.

REPOSITIONING THE PEOPLE PIECE

So how have HR and the people agenda changed since the business began to reinvent itself in November 2004? The simple answer is 'fundamentally'. The list of policies we've redefined and achievements we've made is an indication of just how far we've come.

In the first two years we rewrote 13 of the business's most far-reaching policies. These included our poor performance, grievance and disciplinary policies and our maternity and TUPE policy. Beyond that, we can point to spectrum of achievements and development programmes. Amongst other innovations, we've implemented a new management bonus scheme, introduced unlimited employee discounts and rolled out Peoplesoft in stores. Our training offer has been enhanced by a range of developments, including a new induction process, fitting room training, plus the buying academy, career path and coach training we've already discussed. Together, these innovations reflect a fundamental shift in the way in which we approach people issues. Three years ago HR wasn't adding the commercial value it should have been, but we've worked hard to redress this balance.

This shift cuts right to the heart of our employer brand and HR's role as its champion. I believe HR has two main objectives. The function exists to provide line management with the tools to both improve productivity and increase discretionary effort. This is about reducing costs as well as increasing sales; it's about controlling head-count and benefit costs as well as improving service. Naturally, investment is necessary if people are going to develop along a career path, but this needs to happen within a framework of commercial considerations.

Our new positioning for our people reflects this commercially-minded approach. It says: 'Your M&S people are proud, committed, involved, challenged, valued and fairly treated.' It's worth stressing the notions of 'challenge' and 'involvement'. We want our people to experience some stretch and we expect them to be actively involved with both customers and their colleagues – which, inevitably, translates into high expectations of our managers, as well as our people.

Involvement, in fact, is a key quality in our new employer offer. We've established an extensive grass-roots consultation forum through our business involvement groups (BIGs). These ensure that more than 4,000 people on the shop floor are actively involved in shaping the direction of the business by feeding into key decisions.

The building blocks of this initiative were here three years ago. However, at that time consultation didn't extend far beyond the quality of the tea in the staffroom. We've now taken this to a whole new level, shaping some of our most important changes, including our pension plans, from the bottom floor up. Staff are now able to ensure that their feedback about the things that most concern, including their terms and conditions, reach more senior ears than just those of their immediate manager.

An Employer of Opportunity

Where are we now, then? And, more importantly, where are we going next? In simple terms, I think we have made good progress and addressed the major people challenges that we faced three years ago. We're now entering the Broaden phase and are pursuing our aim to become an employer of opportunity.

Importantly, our offer to employees is now couched in terms of a contract. We have developed from an adult–child relationship with our people to an adult–adult one. We ask our people to commit to life in the new emboldened and commercially-mature M&S with all the expectation of great service that this entails. Then, in return, we promise them what is arguably the most compelling ten-point promise in retail.

Let's end on that. Join M&S and we will:

1.   make you feel valued and *proud* to work for M&S;

2.   *reward* you well against our retail competitors;

3.   make sure you have *inspirational, effective line managers* who value and support you;

4.   tell you how the company is doing;

5.   give you opportunities to share your *ideas* on improving the business;

6.   *listen* and deal with your issues and concerns;

7.   *train* you thoroughly to do your job;

8.   offer you *career opportunities* and support to take advantage of them;

9.   tell you how you are doing;

10.   treat you fairly, using modern, transparent employment policies.

7

Learning the Lessons of History – All Over Again

Lou Manzi
Global Head of Recruitment, GlaxoSmithKline

You never get a second chance to make a first impression. But in 1989 when SmithKline Beckman merged with Beecham Laboratories, we were able to overturn that old saying. Little did we know that ten years later we would put into practice what we'd started to learn in 1989. History may not always repeat itself, but I think it's a great teacher. The trick is discovering exactly what lessons you need to learn.

When two multinational drug companies merge, the opportunities for brand development are practically unlimited. In the late 1980s, SmithKline Beckman was a formidable power in the US pharmaceutical and healthcare industry. The time was right to match strengths with a partner that could increase our market share in the UK and Europe. Beecham stood up to every test. The merger created one of the largest pharmaceutical companies in the world. Enter SmithKline Beecham.

A Golden Opportunity

Recruitment saw the merger as an opportunity to create a brand of its own – a recruitment (employer) brand. This was a comparatively new idea that many companies were only beginning to consider. At that time, I was the head of a forward-thinking, marketing-driven and very creative recruitment team. They also had boundless energy – which, as things turned out, was very fortunate.

In the new SmithKline Beecham, we focused on both building an image in the minds of our current workforce and communicating to the new and larger employee market we'd just joined. We had to convince our current employees and all future candidates that this was – and would be – a great place to work. All companies have a brand. We wanted to ensure that our new brand would be created by design, not accident. It was an opportunity to have a say in who we wanted to be and what we wanted to become.

As it turned out, what we wanted to achieve would be far more complicated than we ever imagined. Initially, we gave little time or thought to how many people our plans would touch. With the scale of changes we had in mind, the input of a few recruitment gurus alone would not be enough. Collaboration was essential – and a relationship with a recruitment solutions provider was already in place.

WHOSE JOB IS IT ANYWAY?

In 1989, branding felt like an alien concept within the recruitment community – best left to those with something to sell to customers. Very simply, employer branding is ensuring that the corporate brand is in sync with the 'people' brand. The messages of what we want our business to become must be aligned with the way our leaders and our people behave.

Looking back, we thought responsibility for the project belonged to recruitment and our external partner. Actually, the challenge probably belonged to the corporate communications group. What we didn't really see was the bigger picture. On the one hand there were the interactions and day-to-day dealings our recruitment teams had with the external candidate community. On the other there was the relationship with Hodes. This put our recruitment team right in the middle of everything, including what turned out to be a war-zone.

I was confident that we had the team with the right skills already in place. We had sales, marketing, finance and HR experience all together. Each of them had recently been candidates in ours and other companies. They certainly shared the candidate perspective and were able to view candidates as customers. We really took the branding concept on board and were convinced we had something to sell to the outside world. We just needed to convince the internal business mechanisms that what we planned to do would meet the needs of the business.

As head of the team, I knew my job was to challenge and inspire these talented people – and hope that their capabilities and competencies would work on our behalf.

THE IMPORTANCE OF EMPLOYER BRANDING

All companies talk about their quest for talent and the importance of recruiting the talent of the future. Over the years, I've seen many companies lose a great opportunity to attract the right people because they were unable to develop or even maintain their brand. Branding is not just about advertising. It's about every thread of their existence. A company with a great brand has a distinct advantage over those that don't. Our team knew we needed to get the right people in the right jobs to compete effectively in the marketplace. By developing the right recruitment brand, we would create a legacy – ensuring there was a never-ending supply of talent who would make a positive difference to the bottom line.

We wanted to be sure that our branding initiative was not just seen as an HR function. We needed to engage employees from all levels to create and sustain the brand. When candidates form an opinion about what it might be like to work at GSK, they need to have that opinion validated when they visit us and meet our people.

Articles on recruitment branding started to appear in the late 1980s. The whole idea was gaining greater acceptance. Our biggest challenge was convincing our partners in corporate communications that we knew what we were doing. We also wanted to own part of this process. In the past, a task like this one fell outside of recruitment and in the shared areas of marketing, corporate identity, corporate communications and HR. We knew that our success depended on creating an integrated approach for the entire organisation. If it were to be aspirational, it had to be straightforward and understandable to anyone who vocalised it.

HINDSIGHT IS 20:20

Looking back to those days in 1989 and 1990, it is amazing how empowered and capable we believed we were. We had taken the initiative to create the company's first recruitment brand. We were convinced that our new organisation held the most promising future for current and future employees. We all knew that if the recruitment function was going to have a major impact, we would need to do something drastically different and get candidates to notice the new company.

We also knew that we would be able to work with members of the corporate management teams as well as many of the hiring managers who really understood the importance of branding. It wasn't about just another tag-line. The brand really needed to state who we were and what we stood for to candidates and to our employees as well. We had a fair number of successes along the way, but invariably we spent most of our time arguing with constituents about what branding should be and who should own it. While the ideal world would have had a corporate brand everyone could own and aspire to, we created an employment brand – for which there was little or no appetite.

A PROPHET IS NEVER ACCEPTED IN HIS OWN TIME

We all knew that we were doing the right thing. But that didn't eliminate the challenges we faced. At the time, most people viewed branding as a rather ho-hum generic term. How could an organisation deliver a brand? Isn't that usually left to products? The consulting team spent many nights and days working with us. Eventually, we took a rather broader view and saw employer branding as the way our business positioned itself internally and externally. If recruitment was the face of the business, we had to be aligned. This created an entirely new discussion within our team around candidate care. Our people had to live up to what candidates read about us in our brochures and saw in our ads. While many of our colleagues in the new company weren't convinced of the journey to which we were committed, our team had no doubts.

One example of how powerful a new brand could be stands out in my mind. I was involved in on-campus interviews during this time. Candidates spoke about how they would like to work with the new breed of lawyers from SmithKline Beecham. We went on to complete the screening interviews. Never did I tell them that we were actually a new pharmaceutical and consumer products company.

Naturally, there was a bigger challenge ahead – how do we ensure that 45,000 employees throughout the globe practised what we preached? Most branding experts will tell you that you need to sell your brand to your employees before you can sell it to your customers. We could create the most impressive brand promise with all the bells and whistles and then try to sell it to our customers but, unless our own employees believed in it, we would be wasting a lot of time and effort.

Many of those employees had their doubts. Some were delighted with the merger and some were sceptical. While a branding initiative may take months, the underlying maturation of that brand and the ongoing change of behaviour may take years. We had to start somewhere.

We spent a lot of time in focus groups with current employees – many of whom had been with the company for some time. Some were happy about the merger and some were not. I learned long ago that 'no now doesn't mean no forever' and I was not going to be dismayed by people that weren't totally on-board. We looked at new starters – many of whom had just come out of university. We took a cross-section of employees, making sure we captured the perspective of scientists, marketers, functional staff members and even employees who had left as part of a voluntary redundancy programme. Our plan was to leave no stone unturned and to be certain that we captured as many feelings and beliefs as we could. At every weekly staff meeting, we looked at the insights from focus groups or the results of surveys from new starters.

This initiative was bigger than we anticipated. We needed the data to be honest and unbiased. Information was captured as quickly and concisely as possible. We chose not to rely on our recruitment staff to do the intake. We didn't want to 'lead the witness' or influence those in the focus groups. In all cases, we used non-employees to collect the data. This took longer than we had anticipated, but we were certain that the information that was being gathered would reflect the honest opinions of staff and candidates alike. We wanted to create a new brand that truly reflected outside and inside beliefs.

We were betting everything we had in our recruitment arsenal that our plans would work. While there were many difficulties in trying to align 45,000 employees, we were delighted by the number of new starters and external focus group participants who wrote letters of encouragement to the team, congratulating us on our efforts. They were mostly happy to be part of the initiative and rarely– almost never – did I get a nasty letter or phone call telling us that we were out of our minds. This was new ground, and most of the employees and candidates taking part saw our work in a positive light. Their responses kept me going.

UP OR DOWN?

We debated many times whether this process should be a top-down or a bottom-up initiative. It was essential that the CEO and senior support staff be unwavering. We were fortunate to have leaders who empowered employees and valued their drive. These leaders always valued the HR function and saw recruitment as essential to the future. They embraced the work that we started and paved the way for our progress. They ensured that our initiative made it to the CEO's agenda, helping us forge a vital link to the strategy of the new organisation.

In creating our recruitment brand, we were focused on dealing with candidates and new hires – and on determining what their perceptions were about the new company. The methodology that we used was a rigorous process whereby we asked candidates what values and mores they expected from a company like ours. Did their observations of our behaviours reflect their perceptions? Our recruiters were actively involved in this process. They worked hand-in-hand with our partners at the consulting group trying to get the customer perspective and building a brand that reflected not just the employee perspective, but also those of our customers and candidates.

BUT DID WE LEARN ANYTHING?

A project as complex as this one has to teach invaluable lessons. There are things we could, and perhaps should, have done differently. Changing mindsets and opinions is not an action; it is a process that needs buy-in and engagement. Command-and-control decision-making wouldn't have worked. Change needs variable speeds. The hardest thing our team had to deal with was old opinions and stale mindsets. The new culture we were trying to create needed more understanding, an exchange of concepts and modalities, not a mandate to make something happen.

With hindsight, it's clear that process determines product. I believe that we could have focused more on the process rather than on the execution of the product. We were very intent on creating the brand and we might have been better prepared if we had taken a bit more time upfront planning the process, rather then just letting it evolve. Regular and consistent communication to the management teams and our constituents would have resulted in less confusion and a clearer explanation of our goals. There were no specific plans for communicating our efforts across the organisation. Sometimes, it was a memo or a newsletter or different communications to a variety of people. Having thought about this many times, having a regular communication schedule and a rigorous process to address issues and concerns from employees and managers would have worked in our favour.

We convinced the company that the recruitment teams were leading many or most of the external facing activities and our recruitment brand, 'Realize Your Potential' was an idea to be reckoned with. Luck never hurt any project, and we were lucky to have had the support of several of our corporate communications colleagues. Their efforts made an enormous contribution to our success.

When I think what we achieved nearly 20 years ago, the excitement is still tangible. Many people have asked me if I would do it all over again. 'Absolutely' is the answer.

Be Careful What You Wish For

Ten years later, I got my chance. Glaxo Wellcome and SmithKline Beecham merged, and the recruitment branding process started all over again. It never occurred to me that the work we began in 1989 was just a practice run for a branding exercise that would be bigger than we had ever imagined. Would we be able to apply the lessons that history taught us?

In the late 1990s the world was exposed to stories that Glaxo Wellcome would be taking over the US pharmaceutical giant SmithKline Beecham. The media buzzed with speculation, and we would often wake to to new articles in different international newspapers that hinted at a major pharmaceutical takeover. Would SmithKline Beecham take over Glaxo Wellcome or would there be other giants in the deal? After some on-off attempts, in January 2000 a new player in the global drug market – GlaxoSmithKline – was formed.

The merger was billed as a merger of equals – a title validated by the composition of the management teams as well as the board of directors. Each company had a 50 per cent representation. There was actually a selection process for the top 1,000 positions at GSK, with an external consultant overseeing the selection and appointment process of vice presidents and above.

The corporate executive team headed by the new CEO, J.P. Garnier, also comprised representatives from both legacy companies. Although employees from both camps were certain that they were taken over by the other, everything was done to ensure that this was a new company, with a new culture and a new philosophy. We took the best from each to create something new and better. This was an attempt to show that the whole is indeed greater than the sum of its parts.

As for selection, each employee in their respective legacy organisations needed to apply for a role in the new organisation. There were no guarantees. The selection and appointment process was overseen by representatives from an external consultancy. So while each of us was working in teams trying to build a new brand and a new organisation, most of us in senior leadership positions were still doing our old jobs. We were also worried about whether we'd even have roles in the new GSK.

The new CEO oversaw the selection process for the corporate executive team (CET). Our consultancy was also involved in the selection of the new executive team, ensuring that there was equal representation of leaders from both legacy organizations. Fair? Yes, but a lot of capable people left as a result of this process.

All this is a difficult enough process for any business, but our work was by no means over. Not by a long shot. We needed to create a new and better culture – one that wasn't a blend of both companies. It had to be new and different, with its own set of goals and behaviours. If you've ever thought creating a recruitment brand was difficult, you can easily imagine how pleased I was not to be part of the culture team.

The newly appointed senior vice president of HR, Dan Phelan, had overseen the earlier branding initiatives at SB. He let us know that, before the merger, no attempt had been made at employee or recruitment branding on the GW side. Dan went about creating numerous integration teams comprising legacy GW and legacy SB employees. He continued to champion the branding initiative that we were leading. Due to the success of our efforts the first time around, we were given *carte blanche* to do it again.

A merger integration team was formed to create the new GSK recruitment brand. Those of us from SB had the advantage of the lessons we had learned ten years earlier. There were also recruitment professionals from GW who had never undertaken anything like this and had an unbiased approach to branding; they were able to come to the table with an open mind. There were those on both sides of the table who thought that they were being acquired by the other side and were far more sceptical. We went about the task in much the same way that we did ten years earlier. Our relationship with the recruitment solutions company we used before had been a successful one, so we asked if they would be willing to have a role in our newest initiative.

YOU CAN'T COMMUNICATE TOO MUCH

A merger of equals comes with its own share of preconceptions and even misconceptions. The media also had its own interpretation of what was happening or what would be happening. Our new CEO and the CET made a decision: it was only fair that our own employees have access to quick and accurate communication. To that end, the corporate communications team did a stellar job, ensuring that any and all decisions were communicated to every employee through the company's intranet, bulletin boards and video communications network.

Knowledge and accurate information is a gift that many of us take for granted. I have a saying: 'What's worse? Not knowing or finding out?' Not knowing is much worse. We may not always like what we hear, but accurate information gives us the opportunity to make better choices – for ourselves and for others. During all my 23 years with GSK and its legacy companies, I have always had access to the information that I needed or wanted. I may not have liked what I heard, but I was never left in the dark.

Once all technicalities were approved by the UK and US legal teams and their respective governments, nearly 110,000 employees needed to begin working and acting like GSK employees. Easier said than done, but that would be another chapter.

The creation of a new company and the need for a new culture set the stage for a robust, identifiable and connected brand identity. Working in concert with the communications team and our consulting partners, we were guided by the belief that a recruitment brand would help us build and nurture a new culture – one that would enable the best people to do their best work and support the entire organisation in delivering its brand promise. In principle, we believed that we could have a positive impact on the entire organisation and give GSK a competitive advantage.

WHAT HAVE YOU DONE FOR ME LATELY?

By the spring of 2005 the competition was starting to develop their own brands. It was clear that at GSK we needed to take an additional step to push ourselves even further into the lead. During a conversation in London with several of our partners, we came to an agreement that most of our competitors – ourselves included – were playing it too safe. We were part of big Pharma, and we were definitely acting the part. It wasn't in our best interest to be bold – or so we thought.

We began to consider our situation more carefully. What if being bold was the secret? Should we do what none of the competition had done and take a chance? What did we have to lose? In June 2005 the HR leadership team gathered for one of its quarterly meetings. Recruitment had a spot on that particular agenda, and we were proposing an enhanced recruitment brand. We called it BAPB. Bold, Authentic, Pragmatic and Breaking the Mould!

I remember that meeting as if it were held yesterday. I even recall where everyone sat during our presentation. Most importantly, I remember being stunned when everyone agreed with our proposal. We anticipated that the HR leaders from the businesses were going to push back or even suggest a toned down message. I was shocked when there was total agreement on the part of the leadership team to take a quantum leap and move forward with BAPB.

So what does BAPB stand for? Bold in how we take ourselves to the marketplace, including the ideas we express and the tactics we employ. Authentic, ethical and transparent in how we conduct our business. Pragmatic in a point of view that enables us to speak directly and openly in all communications. Breaking the Mould with ideas, actions and successes that set us apart.

We were actually going in a completely new direction. Steps like this are risky, but our competitors were closing in on us, and we had no choice but to take the chance.

Making our Messages Count

Sometimes, it's not just what you say, but how you say it. We wanted to make ourselves heard in the recruitment marketplace. The real problem we faced was perceptions. Big pharmaceutical companies were seen as being much of a muchness, particularly when it came to career opportunities. So we went back to our recruitment solutions partner and asked them to help us develop an employer brand that would really set our organisation apart. They worked closely with GSK to develop a distinctive tone of voice for the entire business

– a way of communicating that would give maximum impact to everything we had to say. It would further align corporate communications, brand reputation and HR communications.

This tone of voice was built on extensive research. We were able to use it to develop a portfolio of messages and concepts. To make sure we'd successfully captured the spirit of the organisation, we shared our work with people from within GSK, as well as external parties.

We held a number of focus groups with business leaders and hiring managers, where they were asked to assess, critique and customise the creative messages. Recruiting professionals were invited to discussion groups to validate the concepts, formats and messaging. We also spoke to over 100 people at a recruiting event for diversity candidates, and employee surveys were conducted to identify key copy points and relevant concept platforms. Our research found a positive response. Recruiters and HR teams across the business were quick to embrace these new ideas. And the results speak for themselves. The time to source candidates has been reduced by 38 per cent to 44 days. More than £3.2 million has been saved in headhunting fees. The work has helped recruit people into everything from IT to R&D. And even when the ads went live in markets where GSK wasn't well known as an employer, we enjoyed real and measurable success (see the appendix below for a 'before and after' view of our recruitment advertising campaign).

And so – we did it once, we learned from our mistakes and we had the chance to do it again. We also learned that sitting on your laurels and boasting only invites the competition to nip at your heels. And that's exactly what made BAPB an award-winning approach to recruitment branding.

We are still on the road to achieving our aims. We've had our successes and our setbacks and we've learned a great deal from both. Although it's taken awhile, I believe that GSK will go on to become one of the best integrated and best managed pharmaceutical mergers that this generation has seen.

An Afterthought

Many years ago my parents and teachers told me that during my career I would work with many people that I liked, trusted and with whom I'd become friends. They also told me that I'd work with a handful of people that I didn't like – but would teach me a lot. They were right on both counts. Working with people who believe in your task is easy. Working with those that don't is much more difficult, but provides you with information and a perspective that are crucial to your mission. We're often too quick to cast aside people whose opinions we don't share and who don't value our work. After all, they don't make our jobs any easier. But the truth is that different, or even conflicting, viewpoints result in a much better product.

Appendix: What a Difference a Merger Makes

Figures 7.1a–c show the recruitment campaign as SmithKline Beeecham. Figures 7.1a–c show the campaign ten years on as GlaxoSmithKline.

Figure 7.1a   SmithKline Beecham recruitment advertising campaign (1)

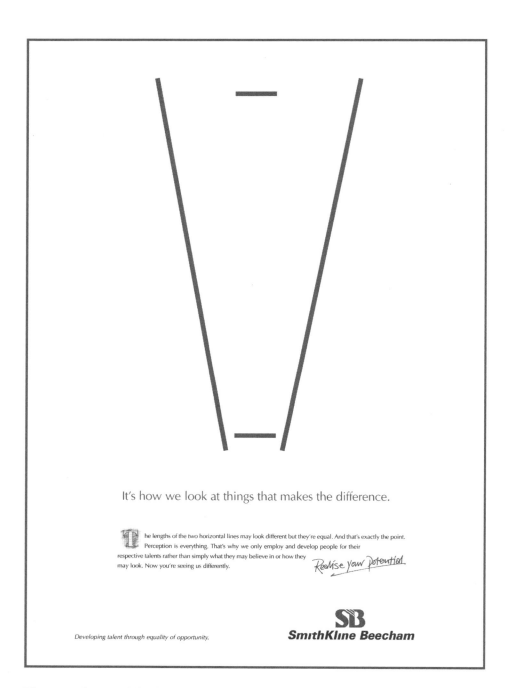

Figure 7.1b   SmithKline Beecham recruitment advertising campaign (2)

Figure 7.1c   SmithKline Beecham recruitment advertising campaign (3)

Figure 7.2a   GlaxoSmithKline recruitment advertising campaign (1)

DON'T BLAME US.

Graduate Opportunities: IT, Engineering, Production Management, Statistics, Science, Sales and Marketing, Finance, Purchasing and Regulatory Affairs

When you've turned the page and missed out on the huge variety of roles that are available at GSK, it'll be too late. Too late for us to tell you that in addition to all the exciting scientific opportunities that you'd expect from one of the world's leading research-based pharmaceutical and healthcare companies, there is a wide range of other, non-scientific graduate opportunities you can move into, in areas ranging from IT right through to Engineering. We would offer our sympathy – but you're probably about six or seven pages away by now.

THE TIMES
GRADUATE RECRUITMENT
AWARDS 2007
'Graduate Employer of Choice'
RESEARCH & DEVELOPMENT

If you are still here though, we imagine you'll be amazed at what's on offer. Visit our website for the most up-to-date opportunities at www.gsk.com/uk-students

Together we can make life better.

gsk.com/uk-students

All data processed in accordance with the provisions of the Data Protection Act. GSK is proud to promote an open culture, encouraging people to be themselves and giving their ideas a chance to flourish. GSK is proud to be an equal opportunity employer.

Figure 7.2b   GlaxoSmithKline recruitment advertising campaign (2)

SOME ENGINEERS DON'T HAVE A CLUE.

Would you believe that there are still a handful of engineers out there left in the dark when it comes to our graduate opportunities? But here's some news that'll light up their lives – our graduate engineers get to work on some of the most exciting challenges in the industry.

And we pack an awful lot into our three year Technical Development Programme. We treat them to a variety of roles spanning vastly different parts of our manufacturing operations. Of course, such regular rotation means our graduates have to adapt quickly to working with new teams. It also means they get to meet new people at every turn, and develop a wide range of

professional expertise across our business. What's more, because we actually let them take ownership of their projects, our graduates can go home at the end of each day knowing exactly how vital they are to the continued success of our pipeline. But we'd like to think that you're one of the bright sparks who knew all that already.

There's still plenty of other stuff to tell you. Simply visit www.gsk.com/uk-students to find out more. We have graduate opportunities for Engineers: Process, Chemical & Pharmaceutical, Mechanical, Electronic/Electrical and Automation, plus a variety of other scientific and numerate disciplines.

Together we can make life better.

gsk.com/uk-students

gsk GlaxoSmithKline

Figure 7.2c   GlaxoSmithKline recruitment advertising campaign (3)

8

Solving a Crisis Out of a Drama – The Passion Behind Social Responsibility

Sally Jacobson

Group Director, Human Resources, London & Quadrant Housing Trust (1987–2008)

The L&Q Group manages over 57,000 properties in the UK for affordable rent. It also provides access to low-cost home ownership and builds housing for sale. Founded in 1960, L&Q employs more than 1,100 staff and works, with charitable status, with over 90 local authorities in London and the South East.

Turning Principles into Purpose

Quadrant Housing Association was set up in 1963 by a group of young professionals who had met at university. Calling themselves the '1958 Dining Club', they shared a strong sense of social responsibility and all were passionate about improving the state of housing at the time. Almost 50 years on, these motivations and principles are still at the heart of L&Q's employer brand.

The circumstances surrounding the creation of the L&Q Group still shape our employer brand today. The L&Q story gained real momentum with the BBC docu-drama *Cathy Come Home*. This hard-hitting play, directed by Ken Loach in 1966, abruptly brought the issue of homelessness in the UK to the public consciousness.

The drama told the story of a young couple: Cathy and Reg. Initially, their relationship flourished. They had two children, Reg was in regular work and they moved to a modern rented home full of hope for the future. However when

Reg loses his job after being injured, these hopes soon evaporate. Cathy and Reg sink slowly into poverty and have their dignity eroded as they're visited by bailiffs and shuttle between shelters and illegal squats in empty homes with two young children in tow. Finally, Cathy and Reg have their children taken away by social services. Despite all the parents' energy and efforts, the family is torn apart by the lack of permanent housing.

The first time it was broadcast, the play was watched by 12 million people, a quarter of the British population at that time. Never had a TV drama had such an impact. It broached issues that were not widely discussed in the popular media, such as homelessness, unemployment and the rights of parents to remain with their children. In turn, this highlighted the social injustice of poor housing and raised the profile of homelessness, squatting and the activities of shark landlords like the infamous Peter Rachman.

Determined to provide practical solutions to these social injustices, the volunteer members of the '1958 Dining Club' started an organisation to provide quality housing for people in housing need. In essence, this is what we still do today.

The Idea Gains Ground

The new venture, which became known as Quadrant Housing Association, was initially focused on south-east London. Indeed, the name was inspired by the quadrant, a naval navigation device, which reflected the maritime heritage of that part of the capital. However, success came quickly, and it wasn't long before the association had outgrown that corner of London.

In 1973, Quadrant Housing Association joined up with the London Housing Trust to become the London & Quadrant Housing Trust. That point marks the beginning of the rapid ascent of the group. With the 1974 Housing Act, we were able to access government subsidies directed at the sector and we soon became the largest provider of social housing in London.

The Story Today

Although great progress has been made in the last 40 years, our work is as important as it's ever been. There are, after all, still more than one and a half million children living in poor housing.

So where does the organisation stand today? First, let's review the facts. Every 15 minutes of every working day we house another person. We provide homes for 54,000 economically disadvantaged families in London and the South East. The Trust now generates a turnover of £200 million and supports an asset base of more than £7 billion. We also provide low-cost home ownership, targeting key workers, as well as providing supported housing for vulnerable residents.

Behind these figures is an organisation with a clear focus and a strong record. We've grown quickly in the last few years by integrating with other organisations – and this trend is set to continue. The urgent need for new homes – and for them to be well designed, built and run in a sustainable way – has risen to the top of the political agenda. All political parties now recognise that there are insufficient homes being built and that the average salary will not allow for house purchase. As a result, exclusion from home ownership is dividing society in the same way social class did at the time of *Cathy Come Home*. Clearly, the issue of inadequate housing is still alive and well – and we're better placed than ever to tackle it.

Why is Employee Engagement so Important?

Today L&Q is a collaborative, high-performing team of some 1,200 staff. This didn't just happen by accident. Indeed, our people plans have been at the heart of commercial strategy for many years now, and arguably a focus on people has been a part of L&Q's success since its inception.

Our people promise wasn't written down or formalised when the organisation began. Nevertheless there was an unspoken expectation that everyone needed to share a commitment to social justice and tackling housing issues, and this link between our core purpose and personal motivation is at the heart of our employer brand. The original founding members of the Dining Club would recognise the same personal commitment in L&Q people today, and they would immediately grasp the link between engaged, committed people and satisfied residents.

Naturally, engagement in a large complex organisation such as L&Q is about more than a shared set of values. A common sense of purpose and personal motivation is a powerful bond, but, as we came to discover as the organisation evolved, more than this feature alone is needed to engage and unite people.

Arguably, our road to Damascus or moment of epiphany came some years ago during a 'stock transfer'. Stock transfers are the name we give to transfers of housing stock from a local authority to ourselves. They're often complicated affairs involving the transfer of residents and staff, as well as bricks and mortar. On the occasion in question, we didn't pay enough attention to the residents and that meant that we lost the deal and the transfer went to another association.

It was a hard lesson – but we made sure we learned from it. The winning organisation wooed the residents with evidence of high levels of householder satisfaction in other areas of their existing business. This made us think, and we began to debate how we would become 'Utopia Housing Trust', where people were queuing up to be housed and eager to be employed.

The answer was deceptively simple. Only staff who really love their jobs feel able and willing to give fantastic customer care. People who are unhappy, bored or plain miserable will not provide good service to your customers. Yet, as simple and straightforward as this conclusion sounds, it's no easy matter to develop an organisation where the vast majority of people love their jobs. It takes time, dedication and attention to detail. We began by categorising the positive behaviours that we wanted to encourage and the negative and unconstructive ones that we found unacceptable. We made a firm commitment to refuse to compromise on accepting negative behaviour as it demotivates everyone and never produces good customer care.

The Journey from Good to Great

Our first breakthrough came through the realisation that HR can make an enormous difference to the organisation, but cannot implement people change by itself. Rather, we recognised that our role was to empower and enable the charity to move forward in the right direction.

By creating and developing a small, high-performing HR team we were able to do just that. The HR team we have here today is fantastic. We've all worked together for some time and are like-minded and very positive. For our complement of around 1,000 staff, we have a group director, deputy, manager and two qualified HR officers, plus an admin team providing excellent back-up. The training team is also small with a head of learning and development supported by a manager and a small admin team. We work closely together and are fully integrated into the organisation.

One of the ways we've achieved this is by ensuring that there's an HR presence at every interview. With 20 offices in the Group, this is time-consuming; but it's also essential – for a number of reasons. For example, when sitting on an interview panel out in a remote site, we are networking, supporting, mentoring, updating, absorbing the atmosphere and working very closely for a whole day with one of our key players: a site manager. The value of this work can't be underestimated, as it provides an essential link for both HR and the manager and staff at the remote office, as well as a forum for good ideas.

In the drive to fully engage everyone in the organisation, we had to look for some quick wins. In general, we had a strong customer-focused culture throughout our 20 offices, although there were some exceptions. By chance, I picked up a book about excellent service by the American customer services guru Mary Gober – it was to prove a happy accident.

I was instantly impressed by the book. This was something different – all about really empowering staff to want to give fantastic customer service. I contacted Mary Gober in the US, and she agreed to meet me when she was next in the UK. We met and agreed to trial her programme. We were the first to use this method in the UK, and we saw some amazing results. At that time, in 1999, we were experiencing some problems in the maintenance of our homes, so we decided to put our three maintenance teams through the programme. There were around 20 staff in each team. Prior to the training, the team was not hitting its key performance targets, and its target at the time was 85 per cent of repairs on time. From the first month following the Mary Gober training we began to see an increase in performance and the key indicators have never looked back. Our maintenance targets are now 95 per cent on time, and we consistently achieve them.

On the back of this trial, we decided to train every single member of staff in the Gober method of providing exceptional customer service. This took us two years to complete – and, in some ways, it was just a beginning. We continue to train all our new people in exactly the same way and we refresh our existing people every year.

Granted, this was a massive investment in time and money, but we know that it has made, and continues to make, an enormous difference. Looking back, I can see that Mary Gober's training turned a key in our organisation. The training proved that taking responsibility, being positive, courteous and proactive really empowers people and produces massively improved performance.

Gauging Satisfaction

We conducted our first satisfaction survey in 1999 and we were not proud of the results. It told us that only 45 per cent of our people felt valued and recognised for the contribution they made. Our people also told us loud and clear that they wanted us to tackle poor performance. Most organisations have some sort of appraisal system, but I know that most managers can quickly categorise their direct reports as A, B or C and, in some cases, D. However, some managers can be reluctant to deal with the Cs and Ds, and their teams suffer as a consequence. There is general lowering of morale and effort and, inevitably, customers lose out. Conversely, if you are lucky enough to have some As or even A*s in the group, they will not stay with you to work alongside C and D staff. If you appear not to know the difference, why should they make the effort? The results in 2006 were very different, and we have seen steady improvement over the years. Now 85 per cent of our staff feel valued and recognised. There are still areas for improvement, and we are making a major push this year to 'listen more closely' and act upon what we hear.

Training and Empowering Managers: A Good Place to Start

When a prospective employee applies for a job with us, they envisage working for L&Q as an organisation. However, as soon as they're here, the manager becomes the embodiment of the organisation. The manager can make the work experience good or bad. Once employed, people leave managers, not organisations. Consequently, it's easy to see the importance of the manager's role.

So what makes a good manager? Some people are naturally good at managing people; they have a natural warmth and genuine interest in their fellow human beings. But good managers are made as well as born. Strong training is critical to good management, as it builds the confidence that's pivotal to success.

With this in mind, we embarked on a training programme which we called 'Managing the L&Q Way'. All our managers and team leaders attend the core training in the L&Q programme. This is a comprehensive suite of management training that includes development in appraisals, absence management, coaching and mentoring, performance and discipline, and the transition to management. In addition, we have created our own development centre at Roffey Park Management Centre. This allows our senior managers to test their core competencies against UK managers and leaders and formulate a personal development action plan for the future. We also run a Diploma in Management and a Post Graduate Certificate in Leadership, in partnership with one of the UK's leading business centres. These two programmes offer a nationally recognised management qualification accredited by Oxford Brookes University. Acting up experience is also a very useful tool and particularly good for fledgling managers and team leaders. Here, under the guidance of more experienced colleagues, they can practise their skills on the job. Finally, action learning has also proved useful. This is a form of peer coaching and networked support for team leaders, in which the focus is on using presentation, questioning, challenging and listening skills.

Managers need a tool box of skills as different people need managing in different ways. Provided that their performance is strong, it is very important to give managers the freedom to develop their own style. Managers are the main keepers of the culture, and we know that the culture will be different in different parts of the organisation, depending on the manager's style. But, whatever management style people adopt, they need to create a positive 'can do' culture, since, as, without that, customers won't receive the excellent service they deserve. Employee engagement is all about loving your job and going the extra mile – and that begins with the managers, with the initiatives they put in place and with the culture they inspire.

Let's Look at Job Satisfaction

Like most organisations, we have some fantastic people working for us and we want to keep them motivated and engaged. The way in which our managers develop their teams is a key factor in all this. Managers have a monthly one-to-one review with everyone who reports to them. The review is used to measure progress towards goals and targets, but also to check on a number of other areas. We place great emphasis on pre- and post-training evaluation, and training needs are identified and discussed at the review. The manager will then discuss the best way forward with the head of learning and development and put in place a training solution for the individual. Once the training has taken place, a full discussion on the outcome takes place at the review. This ensures that the kind of training intervention chosen was the right one and is making a difference.

The type of intervention may be a traditional training course or it could be job shadowing, job swapping, or arranging to visit another organisation where we know a particular sort of work is being performed extremely well. The manager also updates their direct reports on corporate issues and suggests ways in which they can improve job satisfaction for their staff. We really want to keep our good people on board. We have seen a steady reduction in our turnover rate over the last five years, and it has now settled at around 11.7 per cent. We think this is healthy, as it is good to have some degree of staff turnover.

Keeping Our Staff Motivated

We have to accept that individuals are motivated by different approaches. A young graduate or trainee will not be inspired by the same things as a long-standing member of the team who may have been doing the same job very well for years. We have found that a wide variety of initiatives has helped. Many organisations have excellent terms and conditions, but staff can be unaware of them. Often they are contained within a tome entitled *The Staff Handbook,* rarely referred to by employees except in times of disciplinary matters!

Our approach has been to start from the premise that 99 per cent of people want to do a good job and gain satisfaction from a job well done. In this respect, one of our most important initiatives was to apply for the Investors in People accreditation in 1996. The IIP journey made us join up the corporate plan with the training plan, which, with hindsight, makes obvious sense, although we weren't doing it at the time.

Research suggests that strong high-performing organisations have all aligned training closely to the corporate plan, and ensured that it was fully integrated into their work and responsive to the changing needs of the organisation.

With this insight, our commitment to Investors in People was born. IIP accreditation has been a very useful tool for identifying feedback and generating ideas and suggestions for continuous improvement. IIP is all about building on strengths, developing strategies for times of pressure and uniting our people behind the common goal of creating places where people want to live and love to work.

We have now been re-accredited a number of times, the most recent being in October 2007. The report reflects the 'can do' culture and the high levels of engagement from our people at all levels. It was a testament to the great strides we've made in inspiring and satisfying our people. Assessors were 'impressed with the enthusiastic and positive responses from people at all levels during interviews. It was clear that people are very proud of what they do, feel that their efforts are valued and their achievements are recognised.'

It's our job within HR to ensure that we provide the fertile ground for them to do just that. The question then becomes: how do you create an atmosphere where respect, value and recognition have real meaning? The first port of call is to ask your people, 'What can we do to make your job more fulfilling, more rewarding and to make you personally feel valued and recognised for your contribution?' Of course, you have to be prepared for the answer! We asked our people and received some good ideas.

Let's look more closely at some of the engagement programmes and policies we implemented.

Rewarding our People

OUR PEOPLE AWARDS

Let's begin with the Annual Outstanding Achiever awards. Anyone, a supplier, customer, peer, manager or a colleague from another part of the organisation can nominate someone who has performed exceptionally well in some respect. The award is presented at the 'L&Q Oscars' on the day the whole organisation gets together at the staff conference, The award is a certificate, a special badge and 2.5 per cent of salary. And the fact that many of the winners are nominated by team mates makes the award all the more meaningful.

OUR PEOPLE INDIVIDUAL AWARDS

When one of our people displays exceptional performance that truly reflects the values of L&Q, the manager has the opportunity to celebrate that success. The manager has a budget for flowers, chocolates, vouchers and so on, and can reward the member of staff immediately. This can be a very powerful gesture as it is seen by the team who will be aware of the special achievement. And there can be all sorts of reasons for making these awards, from staying late to help a colleague to going the extra mile for a resident.

OUR PEOPLE TEAM AWARDS

Often a team will really work well together to achieve a particularly successful result. This could be the finance team completing end-of-year accounts ahead of time or maybe a cross-organisational team pulling together the staff fun day to achieve an unforgettable experience. This award recognises the success, whatever its nature, and this is reflected in an appropriate reward. For example, the team might decide to celebrate with a night out. Recognising achievement is very important because success breeds success.

OUR PEOPLE STAFF SUGGESTION SCHEME

One way of listening to our people is to maintain a healthy suggestion scheme, which is exactly what we've done. Every month our regional and divisional teams consider the suggestions. We then reward the best of them with a financial reward of up to £100, or perhaps more if the idea results in a substantial cost saving.

Once a year, at the annual staff conference, we reward the 'suggestion of the year'. The winner receives £250. On average we receive around 20 suggestions a month, many of which have been implemented with good effect. The recent IIP assessors commented on the value of the scheme, noting its effectiveness at cross-fertilising ideas.

OUR PEOPLE LONG SERVICE AWARDS

After 25 years' service, our people receive an award of £500, which is presented at the staff conference. Last year there were six recipients. We also give people with ten or more years' service a sabbatical of up to 12 months.

As we tend to spend less on training for staff who have been with us for some time, we offer these people the opportunity of choice-based, non-work-related development in their own time, for which we give £250. Many of our people have done this and expanded their skills through everything from wine appreciation courses to pottery classes. Learning of any kind is important, and achievement in any area will spill over into work.

OUR PEOPLE STAFF INTRODUCTION SCHEME

One of the best magnets for talent we have is our people themselves. Good people attract good people, and, as it's unlikely that any of our people would recommend an unsuitable employee, we pay them £50 for recommending a candidate.

THE ALUMNI GROUP

Like every organisation, sometimes we lose good people. Unfortunately, these people are often the ambitious ones who are snapped up by competitors after our training has made them highly employable. When this happens, we make a note, and after six months I write them a personal letter, asking if they are still happy with the move. I tell them that we still miss them and that we always have opportunities as we're innovative and growing quickly. If they're happy, we wish them well, but we tell them that when they are ready in the future for a move to give me a call. Last year we had five 'happy returners' – not bad for the price of a stamp! The big bonus for us is that they hit the ground running and understand the culture and ethos from day one.

THE ATTENDANCE AWARD

This award recognises those who have provided a year of 100 per cent attendance. Everyone wakes up at least once in the year with a bit of a cold or even a bit hung over, and the desire to remain under the duvet is strong! In the first year we implemented this award (2004), a retrospective look at sick leave revealed 102 members of staff with 100 per cent attendance. We decided to implement two initiatives: first, an extra day's leave for the recipients to include in their annual leave for the year and, second, as we are quite generous with leave, an offer to buy back five days' leave in the year. In 2006, 390 staff had a 100 per cent record!

Sickness absence is a big indicator of 'corporate health'. We know that if we can reduce the sickness rate by 1 per cent we will have 12 more people at work every day, providing services for our residents. That means a lot in terms of not having to use temporary staff. Our sickness levels have been very low for the last ten years: currently it stands at 1.9 per cent, which includes casual and long-term sickness absence. We also train all our managers in how to manage sickness absence, and they are proud of the results they have achieved. Casual sickness is very damaging to morale and workflow. When our people are on sick leave for longer periods, we have an excellent sick–pay scheme and permanent health insurance. We also keep in contact regularly and offer support in any way it is required.

OUR PEOPLE PROFESSIONAL QUALIFICATION AWARDS

We love it when our people achieve personal success, and we reward their hard work with an award. Working while undertaking a course of study is hard; balancing work, home and study is never easy. As a result, we make sure we celebrate when people gain professional qualifications: the CEO presents these awards at the annual staff conference, and they attract a £100 bonus for a pass and £200 for a distinction.

OUR PEOPLE ANNUAL CELEBRATION

We make an allowance of £100 a head for people to celebrate once a year in their teams. The event can be held at any time of the year, not necessarily at Christmas. We realised that the annual Christmas bash for the whole organisation just wasn't what our people wanted. Nobody really enjoys big corporate events; people want to celebrate with the people they work with every day. The 'war stories' from these events are always worth waiting for.

HR HOT NEWS

Our monthly *Hot News* newsletter includes promotions, new joiners and any 'people news'. This is delivered to every PC in the organisation every month as a quick and easy communication tool. We also have a great communications department that publishes our in-house magazine.

The aim of all these initiatives is to value and recognise our people; to allow colleagues to value their stars and to say 'thank you'. Saying 'thank you' and 'well done' is one of the most important things a manager can do. It means a great deal to the recipient. A handwritten note to someone who has really been helpful in achieving a successful outcome can have a huge impact.

OTHER BENEFITS

We provide some great benefits – and make sure we remind our people about them. We offer a comprehensive range, including maternity, paternity, adoption, parental and carers' leave as well as some innovative ones, such as leave for infertility treatment and for caring for grandparents. These have, by nature, a relatively low take-up, but they produce a strong feel-good factor and help promote loyalty to the organisation.

We have also negotiated some good deals for our people in non-core benefits. We have a strong story to tell in car insurance, personal loans, hospital plan, taxation advice, mortgage advice, reduced RAC membership, wine club, travel service, insurance and many other areas. Externally managed, these deals cost us nothing.

The Power of Communications

In our experience, memorable well-produced communications can have a powerful effect on engagement. We decided to brand all our rewards and family friendly benefits, giving them a distinct identity and packaging them professionally. We then added two booklets to our suite of literature – one on how to develop your career at L&Q and another explaining all about our initiatives on equality and diversity.

This action had an impact over and above what we could ever have expected. Our people loved the easy access and began to realise the variety and extent of the terms and conditions they enjoyed. For example, the booklet outlining how to develop a career at L&Q is very clear about how to put yourself into a great position to apply for promotion. It sets out clearly what is available: job swapping, job shadowing, assistance with studies, secondments and, possibly the best experience, an acting-up opportunity.

Company Awards

'BRANDING HR'

We won a national award for 'Branding HR' which was great for team morale. We were shortlisted for the award alongside some household names and 'big corporates'. The centrepiece of our entry was the branded literature that we've already discussed, although we supplemented this with some pieces targeted at the internal and external audience. Amongst other things, we developed the brand to include a canvas briefcase for new joiners with our logo and awards printed on the front, promoting what a great place to work L&Q is! We issued it to all existing staff, alongside a mug and mouse mat and the family of six booklets. New staff receive the briefcase prior to joining, together with an induction CD and welcome pack. These materials include lots of useful information for new joiners, ensuring that they feel welcome and make the most of our induction programme.

THE SUNDAY TIMES TOP 100 BEST COMPANIES TO WORK FOR

This award has been very important to us. We first gained entry to the list in 2004 at number 67, and we were delighted. In the first year we saved £100,000 on our recruitment advertising budget. We are also the only large London-based housing association on The Sunday Times website.

Over the last five years our staff turnover has reduced and it is now around 11.7 per cent. This reduction has also resulted in big savings. We have seen an improvement in the calibre of applicants, and people have mentioned the list as a reason for applying to work for us. Getting the award was also an external and internal validation of our approach to making our organisation one in which people love to work. We celebrated and gave our staff an extra day's leave as a big thank you.

We have gone on to rise in the list each year and in 2006 part of our group, Tower Homes, gained first place in The Sunday Times Top 100 small/medium sized companies. We also won a special award for 'work–life balance'. This made our people very proud; everyone wants to work for a successful organisation where the old saying 'people are our greatest asset' is really the case. The Sunday Times list is the most rigorous I have ever encountered; it is based entirely on what your people say about you.

FINANCIAL TIMES TOP 50 BEST WORKPLACES

We have also achieved a place in the Financial Times Top 50 Best Workplaces for the last four years. This, too, has gained us recognition, especially within our own sector where we are the employer of choice.

The Audit Commission Inspection

Like all housing associations, we are inspected by the Audit Commission which looks closely at all aspects of our operations. The outcome is measured in two ways: a star rating up to a maximum of three for current performance and an assessment of future prospects. Overall we received a high two stars, with excellent prospects for the future. We were the first large housing association to receive such a high inspection result. Tower Homes, our home ownership division, received three stars and excellent prospects. Interestingly, the Audit Commission inspectors commented on 'the genuine enthusiasm and positive attitude of all the staff they met.' Miserable or disengaged staff would never achieve such a result.

Mergers and Acquisitions

HR plays a unique role in our success in M&A. We are always included in the team pitching for new business. In our sector there are a number of organisations merging, and often there will be competition from other associations. When presenting to the decision-making organisation, we know that there are three groups to influence: the people, the board and the residents. We have found that if we gain the support of the people – the senior team, the middle managers and staff – they will influence both the board and the residents. HR has therefore led the way in helping to gain success in attracting other associations to join the Trust.

In the last three years we have undertaken three mergers, taking in around 400 staff. We have ensured that the L&Q culture has quickly become embedded by core training, gaining confidence early on in the process, and making the incoming staff feel really welcome. I have met individually with every member of staff joining us as soon as the decision is made. This reassures staff that there is a place for them and that their terms and conditions are safe. It is only then that staff can begin to think about the business.

This principle has guided us through all the mergers that intersperse the development of L&Q. Mergers have played a central role in our growth, ensuring that we've grown more quickly than we ever could by organic means alone. And at each point of accelerated growth, our employer brand has helped to channel and focus the expansion. Corporate history is littered with examples of organisations that have lost their distinctive sense of self after a merger or acquisition, but we have managed to avoid diluting our culture as we've grown, not least because our employer brand and our commitment to social housing acts as a focal point during these times.

In our experience, it's very important that mergers are as quick as possible. They need to be swift and effective, as delay causes the business to stagnate or decline while people feel anxious and waste time speculating about what might happen.

We Don't Always Get It Right

Naturally, sometimes new employees, whether brought on board from a merger or not, don't work out, and, when this happens, we have to act swiftly. The recruitment process, no matter how sophisticated, is flawed. Some people perform well during selection and disappoint in post and vice versa. The probation period is taken seriously, and we have around an 8 per cent failure rate. The most important aspect is to move the person out with dignity and sensitivity. This also applies to those people who fail to perform; firm but fair discipline is essential. We still have around 20 of what we call 'reluctant leavers' each year. In some ways, this is to be expected if managers are doing their job well.

So Where Are We Today?

Today we are aware of how hard we must work to maintain and protect our positive employer reputation. It represents a considerable investment in time and effort. So we continually think of new ways to engage and delight our people – an ongoing commitment that has support at the very highest levels of L&Q. After all, this is the only way in which we are going to develop and strengthen the link between engaged people and satisfied residents.

Today we are poised to create more places where people want to live. The need has never been greater, and, fortunately, housing has never been in such a strong position politically. With our people fully engaged, we are in a very strong position to fulfil that aspiration.

9

What's the Deal? The Impact of Legislation and New Technology

David Russell
Group Director, William Hill

William Hill PLC, founded in 1934 and employing over 15,000 people in the UK, and Ireland, is the UK's largest retail betting estate and one of the best-known names in the UK betting industry. It serves hundreds of thousands of customers through a large network of retail outlets, and, in addition, has a substantial telephone and Internet presence through which people can access the full range of betting and gaming services. In 2007 William Hill accepted Internet bets from over 190 countries for over 60,000 events and 30 different sports.

If we began to discuss our employer brand within the business, I imagine there would be lots of questioning looks wondering what we were talking about! However, I'm not sure just how justified that reaction would be. Many employees stay with us for a great number of years; we have no great difficulty in attracting people to work with us; and we have just appointed a chief executive who started as a Saturday boy and 37 years later has made it to the top job. All of which suggests that we must have something of an employer brand even if it isn't known as such.

Old and New

The old vision of our business would be of a smoke-filled, male-dominated, betting shop – probably somewhere that was rather frightening to enter and, even if you did, you wouldn't know what to do when you got to the other side of the frosted glass door. 'Man with flat cap' was likely to be the image conjured up, and the product was all about horses and dogs. Although call centres are seen as rather a modern-day invention, the original William Hill business was entirely conducted over the telephone before the legalisation of betting shops in the early 1960s. In fact, not much happened after that until the arrival of the National Lottery in 1994 when attitudes towards gambling began to change.

Many things happened in the following ten or so years. The opportunity to trade for longer hours came along, first with some Sundays, then with evening opening during the summer period and then latterly with all Sundays and more or less any evening being allowed. These developments dramatically challenged our historic staffing model, requiring us to think about things differently and put greater emphasis on our employment proposition. New products arrived and some of the older ones grew in significance. The increasing importance of football attracted a younger customer. The lottery generated much more interest in numbers betting, and many more sports such as tennis, golf and cricket began to develop a following. Machine-based gaming products, not previously allowed in betting shops, arrived and continue to grow in importance. In fact, across the whole business, gaming now accounts for over 50 per cent of our turnover against the more traditional sports betting products – and this is not as a result of any decrease in sports betting.

The betting shop has changed dramatically and has become much more of a mainstream leisure destination. An increasing number of our customers choose to spend leisure time there in contrast to earlier times when customers might have used it just for an impersonal, and perhaps rather furtive, cash transaction. This has had a significant effect on the corporate view of employer branding.

More recently the implementation of the smoking ban and the establishment of the Gambling Commission as a result of the Gambling Act have brought further challenges. And, of course, as for many businesses, along came a whole new channel, the Internet, which brought with it the potential of a brand-new set of customers – those who may previously have had neither the time nor the inclination to visit a betting shop. So, despite early views that this development would lead to the decline of our high-street presence, it in fact took us off in a new direction with the opportunity for a broader set of customers both within the UK and further afield. The product range grew again with the opportunity to further develop the sporting range and also to introduce gaming products such as poker and blackjack. More recently, the opportunity to bet while an event is actually taking place has grown in importance – for example, in a football context, next corner, next goal-scorer and so on. This participation in 'live' action has captured the imaginations of many of our Internet customers, but clearly, for us, this means having the wherewithal to constantly update prices.

The other significant change from an employee perspective was the arrival of technology into the betting shop, which substantially changed the role of most of our 13,000 front line employees. In the old days (not so long ago), the manager's red pen ruled the betting shop and he used it to calculate winnings and strike out losing bets. This was the key part of the job. Arithmetical gymnastics were vital, and, if we are honest, that ability far outweighed any assessment of the applicant's customer service skills when making selection decisions. This was a real turning-point because, as a business, we had to redefine the roles within the betting shop and, in addition to thinking about how we sold the roles to new people, we also had to tackle the issue of retaining our front-line managers, given that their previous skill-set had become redundant. The enlightened LBO (licensed betting office) manager could see this issue coming and, having just accepted new contracts which required them to agree to a five out of seven roster at an enhanced salary, they understood that the business would have to find a way of driving value out of this role. This saw the birth of the Retail Goal, subsequently adopted across the whole business, and what became known as Competition Beating Service to which we will return later.

The 'Cultural' Change Period

Although we were clear that there were many factors, both external and internal, that required the business to change, we resisted the temptation to announce a cultural change programme – such a tag suggests a beginning and an end and, in our environment, is fraught with danger. Change is not necessarily a race, although it can be time-critical, and so we chose to see it as evolution rather than revolution. The key challenge was to retain the many core elements of the successful past while recognising that we needed to introduce some new ingredients to move forward.

The HR function of some ten years ago was typical of many – reactive, administrative, with limited management skills and not terribly well integrated into the business. The professionals within the function wanted to have a greater impact on the business but were unsure how to achieve it. It was an environment where people were not really high on the agenda. This was disputed by some who assumed that, because we talked a lot about people, this must be so; however, there is a substantial difference between talking and taking action. Even senior directors saw the role of HR as 'feeding the recruitment sausage machine' and 'keeping us legal' – with various definitions of what that actually meant! So the challenge at that time was to give HR a more meaningful role, straddling the twin priorities of delivering the HR basics while ensuring a contribution to the strategic priorities around customer service, business efficiency and growth. If you don't deliver the basics, then, in my view, you never really earn the right to be at the 'big table'.

As a business, William Hill has always had a command-and-control culture – something that is readily understandable when you consider that in 2007 around £14 billion was recycled through the business, delivering a profit of £287 million, most of which was cash! With that statistic in mind, operating to clear rules and regulations makes sense. However, it was also important to find a more inclusive way of moving forward as, in the modern world of work, many people look for a way of making a more interesting contribution than just following the rule book.

The challenge was to retain the cultural heritage of a 'can do' mentality that was quite task-focused and move it forward so that it could make fact-based, rather than personality-based, decisions, become more customer-focused and improve the quality of management across the organisation. On that latter point, William Hill had no difficulty in retaining its key management – in 2001 the average length of service of a top 60 employee (not that they were defined in this way) was some 13 years. In 2007, incidentally, this had grown by a further year. The average manager had great depth – they knew everything there was to know about bookmaking – but limited breadth – little knowledge of what happened in the wider business world. This made it essential to find ways of developing the skills of our long-term managers while, at the same time, attracting new people to the team who knew little about our core competency but had much more experience of the wider management world. In addition there were new skills such as technology, marketing and even, dare I say, human resources that were just not available in the internal skill-set.

Attraction to and Delivery of the Brand

It is worth considering what attracts people to the brand – be they customers (in our terms, punters) or employees. Starting with the punter, we know that location is important and that the community 'feel' and the relationships that develop are a positive attraction. The environment is fast-paced, immediate and tangible, and the William Hill brand has integrity. Good quality of service is also important and increasingly so. In a recent survey, the most important feature was staff service which, at 67 per cent, had grown by ten points over three years. Location, on the other hand, previously believed to be the most critical, was rated at 47 per cent. Speed of service at 60 per cent had grown by 11 points while at the top of the list was friendly service at 70 per cent. Our focus on customer service was clearly important to, and valued by, the punter.

Turning to what attracts employees; well it became clear that there were a great many similarities, around location, sociability, relationships and pace of environment. Additionally employees valued the flexibility of our working environment and in many cases a sporting interest allowed them to bring work and hobbies together – at least to the extent that this is possible. Of course, as with most businesses, there are people who travel a long way to work but much is founded on the local community.

The conclusion we reached, is that, in the case of William Hill, the employer brand and the customer brand are similar in many ways and, at the very least, they share the same foundations: community, sociability and a desire to either give or receive good service. It was also clear that in our business model, in which the managerial pyramid is quite flat and many employees work and live in the local community along with their customers, the people that really deliver the brand and its values are our front-line employees. This being the case, whilst we may not consider that we have an employer brand, in reality it is vital that we are able to attract and retain employees who have similar values to our customers.

Retention

There are, of course, the many usual reasons to focus on retention, but at William Hill there is the additional element arising out of the sociability of the environment. We know that many of our customers visit our shops several times a week and often stay for prolonged periods of time, and they have told us that friendly and consistent service is important to them. They don't want to see a never-ending stream of different faces behind the counter.

The recruitment market in which we fish is highly competitive, and we have to recognise that working in a betting shop or call centre is not necessarily a prime choice. The shops are often highly charged environments with many highs and lows. That said, there is a career path and our LBO managers across our 2,250 locations have an average service in excess of 13 years – so something about the William Hill brand must be keeping them. Additionally, if you look at the make-up of that population you will find they are as likely to be female as male, despite the male-dominated image of our business. Attracting applicants is not generally a problem – we have around 45,000 applicants each year for around 4,000 jobs, most of whom, incidentally, respond to a poster in our own shop windows. Back to that concept of the local community.

In the years prior to this change, we had revamped our recruitment approach and, through an automated screening process via the telephone and the Web, became able to identify people with the core customer skills before they even reached the interview stage. This attempted to remove what I have often described as 'the application form lottery', where line managers sit with a pile of very similar applications and endeavour to apply 'selection' criteria, often more randomly than we would like to admit. The need for arithmetical gymnastics as a key skill had disappeared. The old method of recruitment which involved testing mental arithmetic was no longer appropriate, and we had to give a much higher priority to customer skills.

The real challenge is getting people through the 'six-month gate'. All our research shows that people are at their most vulnerable during their early months, so it is important to make the selection process as good as it can be. That said, however, when we look at engagement survey results we see that employees are at their most engaged during their first year of employment. In fact, they only ever approach that level of engagement again after 20 years service! Clearly there is enormous goodwill towards the organisation at this point, which is not always capitalised upon.

There is a huge upfront training input for new employees. In our call centre, for example, it is four weeks before new employees can go solo on calls, so if you only keep the employee for a few weeks after that it is a huge waste of time and money – not to mention the inevitable negative impact on customer service. Honesty around your employer brand is vital – don't try to portray yourself as something that you are not because you are very quickly found out. Bad things happen in betting shops as well as good. You need to thrive on the variety, the adrenalin and the pace – plus you need the resilience to deal with difficult moments.

From the Red Pen to CBS

With the arrival of technology to automatically settle the bet and the resultant discarding of the previously described red pen, it was essential to give employees something else to relate to. The manager was well aware that his core skill was no longer essential and that something else needed to be the focus. There was indeed some fear within the management population that the business might not wish to afford them any longer. After much internal debate around how best to get value out of the role, a way forward was established.

Thus Competition Beating Service (CBS) was born. Our overriding business goal became 'to get more customers, to spend more money, more often with William Hill than the competition'. This was simple for everybody to understand and something that most businesses would wish to achieve. Whilst we rightly operate in a socially responsible world, it is not unreasonable that we should wish for as large a share of the available market as possible. I imagine there are few businesses that would not see this as a laudable objective. The goal was the 'what' and the Competition Beating Service at the local level became the 'how' and, after much internal debate, the underpinning elements became: friendly service, famous expertise and great in-shop experience (see Figure 9.1). Across the telephone and Internet businesses, the last element became the great gambling experience and thus the whole business, including the functions, became galvanised towards a common goal.

Figure 9.1   The business goal

It is worth considering the concept of famous expertise a little more closely. One benefit in the old world, where the bet was settled manually, was that knowledge of the product was paramount. If you were calculating the winnings on a race, then you had to know a bit about the runners and riders. In the new world, where technology does that job, we were concerned that this skill could be lost and so it became one of the pillars in recognition that it was something of importance to the customer and an area that might not come so naturally to us as we went forward.

There was a further transformation at this time and that was in the way in which we communicated. It's fair to say that our idea of getting things done had been to tell people what to do – there was very little two-way about our approach! Communication had never been a core management skill, but we were encouraged, working with a small agency, to develop a new approach. The starting-point for this was undoubtedly the development of the goal and the CBS pillars, which were developed as a result of a much more consultative model that ultimately led to greater commitment and ownership. No surprise there to the modern thinker!

Employee Engagement

In developing an honest employer brand it is important to have a clear understanding of what existing employees think and which areas are important and motivational to them. Many studies have demonstrated that there is a strong tangible link between engagement and business success. Across William Hill we have examined the link between employee engagement and other business metrics such as mystery shopper scores, labour turnover and absence. Again, we have looked at the sharp end in the shops and the call centre. Perhaps not surprisingly but certainly reassuringly, we discovered that there is a positive correlation between engagement and these KPIs – engaged employees stay longer, attend more often and, perhaps most importantly, work hard to deliver competition-beating service.

Within our business we have learnt that there is a high degree of pride in the brand and that people generally understand the importance of the customer experience. One of the key findings was the value placed on local management – communication from the immediate boss was much more valued (and believed!) as opposed to the corporate message from on high. It takes us back to that point of the local brand, local customers and therefore local management. Our employees see William Hill as their local shop or call centre and not as a great corporate entity.

That said, there is a desire to understand the broader vision for the business and to be clear about how their activities fit into it. The business goal works to some extent, but really must be brought alive at a local level for it to become embedded. One of the great aspects of the goal is that it is not wholly prescriptive so front-line staff have the opportunity, for example, to define what 'friendly service' means for them. There is a huge demand for effective and relevant two-way communication. Good training and support was also seen as an important ingredient. People do look around at the job market – something that we should not be surprised about, given that we are in a relatively low-paid environment. That situation underlines the importance of the employer brand and the need to keep trying to understand what the employees want from us.

What Does The Future Hold?

There have been many changes in recent years that have transformed William Hill from the slow, very centralized and overly bureaucratic 'ministry of bookmaking', into a slicker more agile business better able to respond to new entrants into the market – especially online. Increasingly, responsibility to make things happen has been passed down the line rather than leaving all the responsibility with a relatively small number of senior people.

There is no question that the pace of change will continue. On the one hand, we have a traditional high-street and call-centre business that, whilst mature in one sense, continues to discover new product opportunities and, as a result of this and the changing response to gambling, finds new customers arriving through the door. On the other hand, we have a relatively new Internet-based business. This aspect of our business attracts a much wider customer base – many of whom are new to gambling and seek to participate in the newer gambling opportunities – be they new sports or products such as poker and bingo. BetLive, which allows bets to be placed while an event is actually taking place, is one of the most attractive products in this market. The business is in the process of further transforming itself from one that has a core competence of bookmaking with a bolt on gaming business to being seen as one that is a much broader player in the gambling arena.

The Gambling Commission became effective in September 2007, bringing with it wider regulation but also wider opportunity. We helped shape the Commission – then embraced it. We fully support the principles around fairness, protecting the vulnerable and crime prevention. All our employees went through considerable training in advance of its implementation, although it has to be said that much that has now become legal was already in place.

Our most recent changes have been around the repositioning of the brand itself. William Hill has been regarded by many as a little slow, old-fashioned and not as exciting to deal with as some of its competitors. In research last year we asked some of our customers to describe us. They used words like 'dependable', 'solid', 'reliable', 'honest' but, sometimes, 'boring'. Hence we have developed a new proposition for the brand which centred on 'Thrilling Gambling Action'. This mantra is focused on making people feel that they are at the heart of the action and that, as well as the traditional values of fairness and trustworthiness, the brand stimulates excitement and passion and is much more bold and pioneering. All of this must also move across the employer brand.

The Employment Deal

It is worth trying to summarise the employment deal at William Hill. In simple terms this is what we might call our employer brand. What is it that makes a great many people stay with the business over a long period of time, in many cases developing substantial careers over a lifetime? I think there are a number of key factors which come together. First, it is an exciting place to work. In most businesses the fortunes of the business are tracked on a daily basis but I guess there are not many where money can be lost as well as won with such clarity. At the sharp end, although the full profitability of the business is not necessarily clear, there is no doubt that the majority of our employees are closely attuned with the ups and downs of both the business and the customers in front of them.

It is my contention that one thing our brand has is a strong connection between our employees and our customers. In a way, both parties come to William Hill to make money – the employees to earn it and the customers to win it. The drivers around sociability, location and excitement are there for both. Our business model requires our customers to succeed and our employees to enjoy sharing in that excitement. There is also a strong team spirit at William Hill and whether that is at the shop, the district or team level in the call centre, one thing that comes across clearly is how important that is to people. There is certainly a sense of healthy competition across the business.

Another part of the deal that has emerged over recent years is the clear and motivating business goal. Until we researched it, we did not realise how important this actually is. We are unashamedly a business that is about making money through providing exciting products and excellent customer service. People wanted the clarity and have found it motivational to rally round the pillars of friendly service, famous expertise and great in-shop and gambling experience. All our employment documentation is increasingly branded in this way.

Finally there are great career opportunities. There are many examples of people who have carved out marvellous careers, some stretching to as long as 45 years. Although loyalty to one company is becoming less usual across the business world, I am not left with a sense that this is the case at William Hill. With the development of the Internet business, the continued growth in the UK high street and the development of new land-based opportunities within Europe and beyond, there remain huge opportunities for an exciting, long-term career.

PART III

STRIKING THE RIGHT DEAL

Who Owns the Employer Brand? Asking the Question

Helen Rosethorn

Bernard Hodes Group

From the early days of planning this book, it was clear a chapter on ownership was essential. In all Hodes's work on employer brands the debate around the stakeholder landscape has been a feature. We have learnt – sometimes the hard way – to ensure that discussions about the role of key influencers on the employer brand surface at an early stage, not least because mapping stakeholders, their relationships and networks is an essential element of any programme to define and manage the employer brand. But even with stakeholders carefully identified and bound into the challenge of defining and managing the employee deal, there is the tantalising question of who is ultimately responsible.

It's particularly interesting to see the range of answers that are tabled in response to the question of ownership. In the days when the concept of the employer brand was first emerging we would find HR clients delegating responsibility to those who owned corporate identity and the company logo. Now that a deeper understanding of the concept prevails in more quarters, there are more stakeholders cited in the answers and some consistent themes emerging, too.

The key stakeholders have been referenced earlier in the book – see Chapter 2, Stage 1 of the brand journey: 'Visioning' (p. 27). We decided that it would be illuminating to invite a representative from each of these stakeholder groups to answer the question of who owns the employer brand. We're pleased to have the input of one of our case-study organisations, GSK, once again. However, we also have some new organisational perspectives, notably from Enterprise Rent-A-Car, Royal Mail, the Royal Bank of Scotland and the Ministry of Justice, a tremendous mix of public and private, national and international – if not global in the case of Royal Bank of Scotland – organisations. We have given each commentator complete freedom to answer the question as they wish, encouraging them to illustrate their view with their own organisational experiences. Our biggest disappointment has been our inability to persuade a CEO to bring their perspective to this chapter. We believe that we are partly a victim of timing. The finishing touches of this book were being undertaken in the latter half of 2008 – a very difficult time for many organisations in the face of global turmoil in the financial markets. A number of CEOs agreed in principle to consider contributing, but, when the final push came to commit to some formal position, either they – and/or their corporate communications staff – were reluctant to go on the record. This alone says something about the challenge that the concept of employer branding may face in the longer term – but we shall return to that issue at the end of the chapter. Each contribution below comes from a different organisational perspective:

- HR (Enterprise Rent-A-Car).

- Marketing (Royal Mail).

- Internal communications (Ministry of Justice).

- Corporate communications (GSK).

- Employer branding (Royal Bank of Scotland).

ENTERPRISE RENT-A-CAR

Donna Miller, Human Resources Director, Europe

Enterprise Rent-A-Car is arguably the world's largest car rental company, with a fleet of over 879,000 vehicles throughout 6,900 locations worldwide. Founded in 1957 and privately owned, the company employs more than 64,500 people globally – with over 3,400 in the UK and 190 in Ireland.

Evolution not revolution

In July 2007 the Chartered Institute of Personnel and Development (CIPD) published a report entitled *Employer Branding: The Latest Fad or the Future of HR?* It's a concept that is stimulating a lot of debate.

Essentially, an employer brand is the image of an organisation in the mind of its employees, but it can go much further. It touches key external stakeholders as well, such as potential employees and clients, and can even reach as far as customers. It sits entirely separately from consumer branding. Instead, it's more closely linked with an organisation's corporate identity.

The concept is more important than ever given today's nomadic employee workforce. Gone are the days when everyone spent their entire professional life at one company. The ties that keep us at one place are much weaker, so having an employee brand that can be used as an effective retention tool is a 'must have' in today's job market.

But – and it is a big but – employee brands are like skyscrapers; they can be hugely impressive when finished, but you can't create them without good, solid foundations. An employer brand and the culture of any given company cannot be superimposed on an organisation. It has to *grow* out of it.

When we created the Come Alive brand for Enterprise's recruitment advertising, our aim was to differentiate us from the majority of graduate recruiters. Do you want a boring office job, a thankless junior role, a chance to spend 18 months doing the photocopying? The answer is bound to be 'no', so we wanted to demonstrate that a job at Enterprise is not your 'normal' entry-level position.

Each company has its own corporate identity. This will be made up of various factors, such as company values, internal award programmes, CSR policies and compass points showing a specific approach to doing business. Enterprise was built on entrepreneurialism, so our corporate brand has always reflected that.

The employer brand needs to be closely aligned with that same corporate identity. It's vital that the employer brand that new employees experience stays true to the corporate identity which they were sold at the outset. The experience inside the company needs to be linked directly to the more tangible aspects of the corporate identity – hence the 'from the inside out' slogan of employer branding.

This can make ownership of the employer brand a difficult nut to crack. Who should take ownership of something that should, to all intents and purposes, follow on naturally from an existing corporate identity? The rather annoying (albeit accurate) answer to this question is 'it depends what you mean by ownership'.

If by 'ownership' we mean complete control of its creation and responsibility for its development, then the answer has to be everyone within the company. No one part of the whole should have absolute control of an employer brand. Every single employee has a part to play in creating, sustaining and developing the brand.

However, if by ownership we mean direction and a responsibility to communicate, we can better identify where the buck stops. The worst thing an employer can do is to assume that an employer brand is self-evident and will take care of itself. There needs to be a guiding hand to ensure that everyone has the opportunity to contribute and engage with the employer brand.

This should come from the organisation's human resource (HR) professionals. This is often the area of the business that has the most direct links with employees, so it's often in the best position to take their temperature and use that to shape the employer brand. At Enterprise, our role is to give that message real relevance throughout the company, which means engagement through employee groups and a structured process that keeps us buzzing.

This isn't to say that the HR department should work in a vacuum when it comes to the employer brand. Because the brand is linked so directly with the corporate identity, HR professionals need to work alongside whoever has control over that identity as well. This will often mean working with members of the board or the marketing department to make sure there's a true synergy.

What does this collaborative approach mean for all the stakeholders in the employer brand? Well, it means a great deal of communication. In order to really give an employer's brand some teeth, HR professionals need to be able to gather a great deal of insight and expertise to arrive at a well-defined, well-communicated and consistent brand.

But the end-result is entirely worth it. An employer brand can lead the reputation of an organisation in any given market. It constitutes a vital aspect of the overall corporate identity and can be a cornerstone of establishing the long-term integrity of a company.

ROYAL MAIL

Alex Batchelor, Marketing Director (2005–2008)

Royal Mail is the UK's national postal service, wholly owned by the UK government. With 180,000 employees, Royal Mail collects from over 100,000 businesses, 14,000 post offices and 116,000 postboxes every day, and processes and delivers more than 23 billion items a year to over 28 million addresses, six days a week. Its domestic and European parcels businesses – Parcelforce Worldwide and General Logistics Systems (GLS) – handle some 390 million parcels a year.

There are books on how companies are brands, how companies use brands and on how people are brands. There are books on what brands are, on good brands and on bad brands. There are probably books on how to brand books!

There are mountains of research about how people make choices. How they choose which products to buy, who to marry and who to have children with have all been subjected to detailed scientific study. Yet I can find little on how they choose who to work for and even less on the role that brands play for employees as opposed to customers.

However, at the heart of all these questions about branding are people – people who collect together and live in societies, people who work for the organisations and companies within the societies in which they live and people who buy things from companies, as well as people as individuals, people as part of the collective groups they form and people as 'customers' of the collective groups that exist.

So why have brands? They make choices easier for people. We all have lots of choices; brands make many things easier, cheaper and quicker. People build brands, people buy brands and people also want to work for brands. 'I work for the Royal Mail' is a complete statement (with all the connotations and baggage that brings). 'I work for Interbrand' (as I once did) requires more explanation – who is Interbrand? what do they do? – and my mother struggled to explain that in a way that she doesn't have to with my current job. Some people use their employer as a badge, others don't – but recognition is important. You could see employer branding as simply another axis standing against the customer side of branding. There are organisations I want to be a customer of, there are organisations I want to be an employee of – and there are some organisations where neither applies. During the first week of Terminal 5, I suspect that both British Airways' customers and their employees held remarkably similar views!

Employer branding is distinct from customer branding but still uses many of the same cues and tools:

1. *Visual identity*. What does the company, its offices, its people, its communications look like? Do I feel comfortable here? They say that people decide to buy a house in the first 60 seconds. How similar is our approach to work? I know how different I feel about companies where someone smiles at reception, and this can be much more important than

the freshness of the paint or the size of the atrium. Making people feel welcome is about much more than just appearance.

2. *Targeting*. Who does this organisation need to hire? Where are these people now (for example, in universities, in other industries, working for our competitors)? Bizarrely, when we consider how important we say a good source of talented and motivated employees is there is often little sophistication in how companies target the right groups. A company like Red Bull revolutionised its potential recruitment by targeting entrepreneurial students as a source of growth.

3. *Culture*. How do people behave and what do they value? There have been some great books on the service–profit chain in recent years and some detailed analysis of professional services businesses, like accountants, lawyers and consultants. Many of these businesses claim that they are not brands, but are obsessed with their reputation. In assessing values people always stick with the adage that actions speak louder than words – and many investment banking firms have to accept that their poor reputations amongst women and ethnic minorities are because of their tolerance of poor behaviour on the part of those who make money: given a choice between principle and profit they tend to go for the money. Good businesses learn the lessons from nature and recognise that diversity is a key ingredient of all sustainable environments.

4. *Ownership and ownership of companies*. Someone owns a share or shares, someone is the leader, we all form the collective. Ownership of – meaning responsibility for – things inside organisations is much, much harder.

If employer branding is a branding task, should it sit with the brand and communications professionals? If it is primarily an HR task, then should it sit with them? If it affects the finances of the business should the finance department take the lead? This kind of debate inside companies is misleading. Sole responsibility for ownership shouldn't sit with one function alone. The best companies have leadership teams who share the responsibility for all aspects of their brand, whether for customers or employees.

The tasks of consistency of identity and culture are discussed and agreed, and then each employee has a role in bringing this to life.

It needs measuring, it needs monitoring and it is a crucial element of business success. If a brand is the result of a collective opinion, then it is also a result of a collective task.

The risk is in the cautionary tale of Everybody, Somebody, Anybody and Nobody. Employer branding is an important task and Everybody was sure that Somebody would do it. Anybody could have done it, but Nobody did it. Somebody got angry, because it was Everybody's job. Everybody thought that Anybody could do it, but Nobody realized that Everybody wouldn't do it. Everybody blamed Somebody when Nobody did what Anybody could have done.

MINISTRY OF JUSTICE

Pam Bland, Head of Internal Communications

The Ministry of Justice (MoJ) is a young organisation – formed on 9 May 2007. Its creation has brought together the former Department for Constitutional Affairs and part of the Home Office.

Composed of Her Majesty's Prison Service, Her Majesty's Courts Service, the Tribunals Service, Office of the Public Guardian and numerous other agencies and arms-length public bodies, it is a large and complex organisation that directly employs some 80,000 staff. The MoJ works with an extensive network of voluntary, public- and private-sector organisations to deliver its services, taking the total number of people working with them into the hundreds of thousands.

Our work touches people's everyday lives because we are responsible for: protecting the public, reducing reoffending, supporting a vigorous democracy, ensuring the efficient and effective delivery of justice, and guaranteeing rights and promoting responsibility.

Following our formation, our aim was to create a shared sense of purpose, including values and behaviours, under the umbrella brand of the Ministry of Justice. This includes communicating to our staff, partner organisations, potential employees and the public what it means to work for us – our employer brand.

Having an employer brand is a new concept for the Ministry and a relatively new one in government. In the past a career in the civil service represented a 'job for life' with regular but small incremental salary increases, flexible working patterns and pension benefits. It did not recognise or recruit professionals, but instead valued generalist administrative and policy skills, even in specialist corporate functions such as finance and accounting, IT, HR or communications.

Today the recruitment focus in the service has changed significantly. Now we source senior managers with a broad range of skills and experience, from both the public and private sector.

There is also a move towards recruiting employees with essential skills, such as project management, leadership, and research and analysis. This change is professionalising the service and, together with the transforming government agenda and the new people strategy, is reshaping the culture. The move is from a largely top-down approach to one that engages and empowers people to be active in business decision-making, innovation and driving change.

We are still in the early stages of developing our employer brand. A catalyst for this is our improving recruitment project, which has recently been established by HR. Communications has been involved in the project from the outset, as the guardians of brand and to support the active building of the MoJ's reputation. In addition, representatives from across the business have been brought on board to ensure that we accurately reflect the needs of our agencies and arms-length bodies.

We are working as a team to improve the MoJ's recruitment performance while building our reputation and what it means to be an employee. We know we need to radically change our employer offering in the market and find points of differentiation from our competitors for our attraction strategy.

Interviews with staff have generated a sense of what being a MoJ employee means and where and how within the business this experience is influenced and expressed.

At the same time the Ministry is building its culture, one that is different from either of the large organisations that were brought together. We are changing the relationship between the organisation, managers and employees, moving from being less hierarchical, formal and 'paternal' to empowering people to take more responsibility and to be more collaborative, flexible and innovative. We also want to motivate and engage people to look critically at how we do things, making suggestions and implementing improvements driven from the bottom up. In addition, we are introducing new polices and procedures and opportunities for self-driven learning and development that support our developing culture.

Added to this we are driving up employee engagement with a specific project to ensure that each and every person who works with or for the MoJ has the opportunity to be involved in making it work better.

Our employer brand is an integral part of who we are, and what we do. It's important that it grows with us as we gain a greater sense of our identity. So, in response to the question who owns MoJ's employer brand, I would say everyone who works for or with us, which is quite a challenge!

The reality is if the brand doesn't reflect our common aspirations for what it means and feels like to be a MoJ employee and reflect the experience our working partners share with us, then we haven't got a brand but just a sales pitch. Helping the organisation express the employer brand is the role of HR as the champions of MoJ people, our board as our leaders and communications as the experts in brand development, strategy and engagement.

We have a way to go yet before the MoJ can confidently say that it has a widely recognisable employer brand, but we are definitely on the right path.

GLAXOSMITHKLINE

Elaine MacFarlane, Vice President Corporate Identity and Communications

GlaxoSmithKline PLC (GSK) is the world's second largest research-based pharmaceutical company. Founded in 2000, following the merger of Glaxo Wellcome and SmithKline Beecham, the organisation employs around 100,000 people in over 100 countries.

GSK's consumer brands include Ribena, Horlicks, Lucozade, Aquafresh, Sensodyne, Panadol, Tums and Zovirax.

For me, the employer brand is synonymous with the corporate brand, and touches all aspects of employees' relationships with the company. Ownership lies with the CEO whose values and actions embody the brand and who is its most powerful ambassador. That said, each employee must also assume responsibility for living the brand on a daily basis. In addition, there are key roles in the organisation which can strongly influence the employer brand, and the head of corporate internal communications is undoubtedly one of these roles.

At the time of the merger, I applied for this position not because I was the best qualified candidate (I wasn't), but because I felt very strongly about the influence this role could have in creating an environment in which I and other employees could thrive, grow and be proud of.

Today in GSK, the role of the head of corporate internal communications is combined with the role of custodian of the corporate identity, co-ownership (with IT) of the company intranet, the corporate website, and shared responsibility (with finance, corporate responsibility and the secretariat) for producing the annual suite of company reports for shareholders and other key external stakeholders. Although this is a broad remit, it does, perhaps, promote a greater degree of consistency in how the brand is communicated across multiple stakeholders than would otherwise be the case. Given the overlapping nature of stakeholders and patterns of media consumption in today's environment, I believe there is a powerful case to be made for this approach in other organisations.

So many multinational companies which grow by acquisition struggle to integrate the acquired companies' staff with their existing employer brand and rarely achieve the unity of purpose and culture to which they aspire. In contrast, we were immensely fortunate at the time of the merger to capture our aspirations in the form of a fresh, contemporary brand identity, and make a new start.

This identity remains the cornerstone of our employer brand today and it has come to symbolise what employees love most about our company. These qualities include: the opportunity employees have to do challenging work with other equally talented, passionate and dedicated individuals; our open culture; the medicines, vaccines and consumer healthcare products we discover and manufacture, which enable people to do more, feel better and live longer; and the strong sense of corporate responsibility which is embedded in every part of our organisation.

Every two years, GSK conducts an employee leaders' survey to gauge opinion on employees' views of the company. This survey is an important benchmarking tool for us, as it enables us not only to compare GSK's response with external peer group companies who undertake a similar exercise on a regular basis, but also to compare responses with those of previous years. In almost all cases, the scores from the 2006 survey (the most recently conducted) were well above the mean in comparison with our peers, and for the question on overall satisfaction with our company, our leaders rated GSK higher than any other organisation on the database of 40 comparable peers, which was a terrific result. In addition, 90 per cent of the 10,000 or so managers who completed the survey agreed or strongly agreed that they were proud to be a part of GSK.

Am I satisfied with this outcome? Yes, although this was only achieved through the hard work of many people throughout the company and a very strong commitment to internal communications and engagement by the CEO and corporate executive team.

These foundations have grounded and united us despite the many challenges we face in our industry. As we embark on a broad and deep programme of change to stimulate enhanced growth and transform our company into one which can withstand the pressures of tomorrow's environment, you may ask, 'What next?'

The answer is: we need to retain the essence, or soul, of the company and use our strong sense of trust, collaboration and resilience to sustain us through the next few years. The Greek philosopher Heraclitus said, 'Nothing endures but change', and we are fortunate that change has been such a constant in GSK. There is a strong appetite for this next phase of our future, and our employer brand is fundamental to that effort. Every piece of communication is an opportunity to overtly or subtly communicate elements of our brand, and call this subversive if you will, but I believe it works.

On many occasions, I have asked employees who have been with us for a few months how their experience with GSK contrasts with previous employers. Their responses are always alike. They usually laugh, and say 'There's just no comparison between GSK and where I was before. It couldn't be more different.' These people are the strongest and most powerful advocates for our employer brand, and as long as this continues to be the case, we're in good shape.

ROYAL BANK OF SCOTLAND

Lorraine Taylor, Group Head of Employer Branding

Who Should Own the Employer Brand?

I believe that the CEO of an organisation should ultimately sponsor the employer branding agenda as it is so inextricably linked to external reputation and competitive positioning in the marketplace. In an economy with drastically and rapidly changing demographics, the race for talent from all aspects of society, all ages, all ethnic groups and all genders is officially 'on'. Having an employer brand that is distinguishable is vital to attracting and retaining this talent and to the future success of any organisation.

Once you have the basis of your employer brand, this is not an end in itself. The brand must be sponsored at the highest level within the organisation. First, HR leadership needs to actively sponsor this with the board, gaining their buy-in and seeding it into their communications and everything else they do.

That is exactly what happens in RBS. Here, ownership for employer branding sits within HR, primarily because the solution for the business problem the organisation is tackling lies in the hands of HR – namely, the attraction, recruitment and retention of talent.

Whilst it was recognised that this solution wouldn't progress without cross-organisational agreement, the notion of developing and articulating the employer brand was seen as an answer to the problem. As a result, the influence of HR as a function within any organisation beginning an employer brand journey is a major determinant of success. Indeed, this is reflected in the priority we give employer branding issues within RBS.

HR is by no means the only participant in the journey. Key stakeholders, such as the head of corporate brand/marketing, the head of internal communications, the HR leadership and employees themselves, need to be consulted and managed on an ongoing basis to ensure that the brand continues to evolve and extend its influence. It should then be owned and adopted by all employees. As such, it will then become part of the DNA of the organisation, starting at the very top with clear sponsorship from the CEO and demonstrated in turn by all of the leadership.

That said, it is still important to have someone in the role of head of employer brand to drive its development and to act as its guardian. It is critical to have just one individual who leads on employer branding to ensure that you have the necessary single voice to market it both internally and externally. This individual acts as the conscience and single view of brand from an employee perspective, both existing and potential.

What's interesting is that you will find very few people within any organisation who have employer branding in their job title. So why do so few organisations enshrine the management and championship of the employer brand in a single role? Finding the right person with the right expertise to do the role is difficult. But if we stop and think for a minute, finding someone with the right expertise to do the role *should* be difficult to do. It is a complex and multifaceted role. First this person needs to be operational – to have had hands-on experience in managing parts of the business. This is essential to providing the commercial insight that needs to be woven through decisions on employer brand and, in understanding the two-way deal, through their experience of managing customer-facing teams. Equally crucially, the employer brand champion needs to understand marketing techniques and brand messaging, and have a strong understanding of enterprise communications. Lastly, to be the right person for the role, they need to understand the employee value proposition, so they should also preferably have experience within HR. Clearly, bearing all these factors in mind, it is not surprising that these people are few and far between.

Within RBS, we could not fulfil our employer brand strategy without being positioned in HR – but that may only be right for RBS. Sponsorship from, and collaboration with, the other related functions in an organisation is fundamental to employer branding success. Similarly, it's essential to find the right individual, with the right skills, to fill the brand manager's role.

What are the Key Success Factors for a Successful Employee Brand?

Aside from the question of sponsorship and ownership, it is important that the employer brand has strong roots within business performance as a whole. There should be a direct correlation between employer brand uptake and the health and success of the business itself. To measure this, there are some business metrics that can be used when informing the development of the employer brand and to measure its effectiveness as the business adopts and embeds it. Although this list is not exhaustive, at a minimum your metrics should include staff turnover figures, staff absence figures, productivity, customer satisfaction and any external benchmarks already being used for external employer reputation.

Second, your employer brand needs to be adaptable and seen as an evolving process. If you work in an international, global or diverse business, the employer brand needs to be adapted and tailored for local populations. Brand research should be carried out in all countries/divisions to ensure that it is fit for purpose, or to make any necessary tweaks to make it viable and credible for the local population.

In addition, as Net Gen and the next generation flow into our organisations, they bring with them more expectations around individual choice and what the organisation should tailor for them personally. Employer brands have to adapt to meet these expectations if they are to attract and keep these people within their organisations.

And, finally, successful employer brands deliver what they promise. With this in mind, it is important to map out all the brand touchpoints from a candidate's or employee's perspective. We completed this exercise at RBS and it delivered some invaluable insights. We were able to see where responsibility lay in the organisation for a particular employee experience and who should be part of a cross-functional team developing the employer brand solution.

For example, internal communication was identified as a specific touchpoint and the collaboration between HR and the communications function is most apparent in the creation of our guidelines for all employee communications. These guidelines outline our tone of voice and look and feel for all channels of employee communication. They are owned by the employer brand team and group communications to enable both functions to contribute in terms of expertise, accountability and implementation. Now, with these guidelines in place, we can ensure that each communication to our 170,000-plus employees is on message by ensuring that it matches and articulates the core themes of our brand.

Summary

An employer brand is often seen as a 'nice to have' and something driven out of HR that isn't always understood or widely discussed by the business as a whole. Instead, it should be three-dimensional and viewed as a critical element in the survival and development of a business. Employer brands enable organisations to attract, motivate and retain their people, and help them meet key performance indicators around sales, service and productivity, all of which are key commercial concerns.

If the employer brand is to achieve its potential as a concept, it needs to be actively sponsored by the CEO and leadership team, and adopted and understood by every individual within the organisation. The head of employer brand is merely a conduit for this to happen, not the point at which it all starts and stops.

What Can We Learn?

It's revealing that we have had a consistent answer emerging from our stakeholders. The consensus is that in the day-to-day life of an organisation everyone owns the employer brand, as everyone influences the way in which the proposition between employer and employee plays out. Yet some people within the organisation have more influence than others and, arguably, this changes over time and is linked to key points in the employer brand journey.

Alex Batchelor's tale of 'Everybody, Somebody, Anybody and Nobody' is insightful. Yes Everybody owns it, but is Everybody responsible for getting the organisation to the place of understanding and managing the employer brand? Collaboration is essential, but there are always catalysts to change in life –particularly in organisational life – so who are those catalysts?

HR and internal communications specialists appear to be emerging as these catalysts and see their roles as just that. In our experience, HR plays more of a role in the instigation of an employer brand journey and internal communications' role lies more in the manifestation and day-to-day messaging around the brand proposition inside the organisation as well as its ongoing measurement, tracking and development.

The link between this internal communication activity and the wider corporate communications agenda is perhaps where organisational understanding and consequent behaviours around the employer brand can break down. This is clearly not the case in GSK, which is a major achievement given the global, regulatory environment in which it works. But in other organisations the challenge of satisfying a range of external shareholders and/ or owners can divert from the joined-up organisational behaviour that building a sustainable employer brand demands.

Enter the CEO – as he or she has the power to open this particular door. The proviso is that reputational management is led from the very top; the CEO manages a deal with his or her people to drive organisational success and then creates a leadership environment that engages people in that deal. If all these conditions are met, then truly the planets are aligned! So, yes, everyone does have a stake in the ownership of the employer brand, but some people have more power over its destiny than others and therefore need to take their responsibility more seriously. Collaboration and communication are consistent themes from our ownership commentators, but without leadership the journey can't begin – or continue. The CEO has the first and last word. Or in the case of this chapter, sadly, no word at all! Whilst appreciating that we were searching for a CEO comment in particularly challenging times, with many businesses making cuts in employee costs, perhaps idealistically we wonder why a CEO still cannot stand up and say that the engagement of people is key to their organisation's success – whatever the climate they find themselves operating in.

We cannot conclude the debate on ownership without mentioning one further role. In recent years a hybrid specialist has arrived on the scene in a number of organisations – perhaps in recognition of the particular need to connect disparate stakeholders rather than trying to settle any questions of ownership – and that is the employer brand manager. They are still a rare breed, typically lacking the organisational clout they need and can find themselves held back depending on where they sit – marketing, HR or internal communications. Even with this job title we would hope that an employer brand manager would not say that they own the employer brand. Guardian and activist – yes. Owner – no.

11

From Business Case to Payback – The Challenge of Meaningful Metrics

Paul Crowsley
Bernard Hodes Group

The argument for defining and managing your employer brand is compelling. It is in effect wrapping your arms around the culture and the power of the people factor in your organisation. However, evaluating the bottom-line payback for defining and managing your brand as an employer seems challenging for many.

In this chapter we will examine a number of questions around measurement. For the purist we may appear to be building our argument back to front – but, first, we will look at how the success – or otherwise – of employer brand management can be evaluated. Then we will look at the measurements that can and should be built into a programme to define, evaluate and track an employer brand. And, finally, we will suggest what is therefore relevant and of potential value in building the business case for employer brand management in the first instance.

You will also be able to see just how effectively measurement has been used by the Royal Bank of Scotland (RBS) to manage its employer brand as part of a whole suite of human capital metrics.

Measuring the Impact of Employer Brand Management: From HR Metrics to Brand Measurement

The brand journey described by Helen Rosethorn in Chapter 2 ends with the 'measurement' phase. Perversely, this is a very good place to *start* our discussion of metrics, because the first thing many organisations embarking on such journeys want to know is what this is exercise going to do for them and how they can measure its impact. There is, of course, a huge role for measurement throughout all stages of the branding journey, and this will be discussed later in this chapter.

The idea of metrics in the HR world is nothing new. The importance of measuring 'people cost' has grown with the emergence of the service- and knowledge-based economies of the Western world and the realisation that the asset with the highest 'value' on the balance sheet is in fact people.

A substantial industry has grown up around consultants specialising in HR and human capital metrics, and many large organisations – especially in the US – have adopted rafts of measures and key performance indicators to monitor everything from job offer acceptance time to impact on bottom-line profits. The purpose of adopting this approach is usually to measure either the efficiency of the HR function (a business function which needs to be evaluated as any other) or to assess the overall impact of people on business performance.

Some organisations have chosen to focus on fewer metrics, but to measure them as well as they can and then to celebrate the results (if positive) as a way of reinforcing the value of HR to the organisation. But very few organisations, especially outside the US, implement metrics with any great enthusiasm. In reality, for many employers, measuring standardised HR metrics like cost per hire, quality of hire (if you are lucky) and retention rate is as much as they can manage.

The story of metrics relating to employer branding is very similar. A few employers at the forefront of the field have developed sophisticated measures of, for example, the effectiveness of recruitment marketing or the changing perceptions of their brand. Perhaps the most developed area of metrics is employee engagement, where regular surveys are now the norm for most big employers. Even here, though, good-quality, up-to-date information-gathering is not universal. For most, brand metrics perhaps represents the missing link in the brand journey. However, there are good reasons why this should change.

Employer branding offers an opportunity not only to develop these areas of monitoring, but also to bring them together. It offers organisations the potential to link inputs and outputs, outcomes and impacts and to use the information to continually improve the attraction and retention process.

Moreover, the sheer scale of employer branding, the resources dedicated to it and its huge scope of potential impacts demand that a proper monitoring system is developed. As noted in the recent CIPD paper on the subject,[1] employer branding reaches everywhere: it's not just traditional HR metrics that will be affected; new kinds of measures are needed – for example, the level of ability to source directly because of brand strength rather than through third parties. And the wider impact of employer branding – potentially all the way through to the consumer and bottom-line profits – has to be assessed.

But what do we mean when we talk about measuring *impact*? Let's start with some definitions.

What Do We Mean By 'Impact'?

When we talk about analysing impacts, we are really trying to answer the questions 'What are we *ultimately* trying to do here, and are we achieving it?' and 'What effect is this having overall on our organisation?' These are questions that will be most dear to the hearts of the people paying for employer branding activities, and of the executive board.

Related to this are subsidiary questions, weighing up the ultimate impact against costs and other inputs. Like any other HR activity, employer branding as an activity should be constantly reviewed and improved, asking 'Are we doing this efficiently and effectively?' and 'How could we do it better?'

These could perhaps be seen as the *ultimate* impacts of employer branding, and these are the focus of this section. Those involved in employer branding sometimes consider changes in brand perception or improvements in an employer's ranking in 'best employer' surveys as impacts. However, we'd like to suggest that these are perhaps best seen as *intermediate* or *process* impacts or *effects* In other words, these are means to other ends rather than ends in themselves (more of this in the next section).

The model in Figure 11.1 summarises the logical chain of events in implementing an employer brand management programme and illustrates where each type of measure fits in.

---

1   'Employer Branding – The Latest Fad or the Future for HR?', CIPD, 2007. Available at: http://www.cipd.co.uk/subjects/corpstrtgy/empbrand/_embrltsfd.htm.

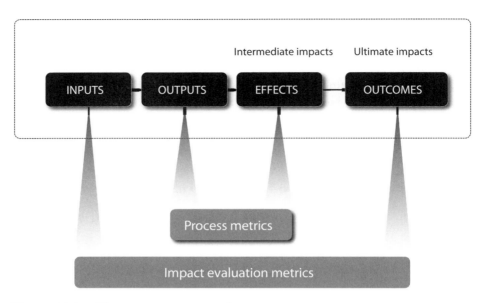

Figure 11.1   The measurement cycle

The employer branding process can be seen to have *measurable*:

- *inputs* (including money spent and time exerted);

which lead to:

- *outputs* (advertisements placed, communication channels used, behavioural workshops run);

which cause:

- intermediate/process impacts or *effects*:

    - first, changes in perceptions of the brand,

which will bring about:

    - changes in attitudes, motivations, propensities, behaviours and intended behaviours,

which together lead to:

- ultimate *impacts* (or *outcomes*) – the results of the expenditure or return on investment, as experienced by the organisation.

We are not suggesting that all organisations will wish to develop measures in all of these areas. Many, for example, may feel that measuring 'outputs' is not a priority for them. Rather, the important point is to recognise the potential scope of metrics that could be used.

It's worth noting here that, despite talking of one event 'leading to' another, in practice evaluating the causal chain of activity and outcome isn't that straightforward. We'll examine this in more depth later, but initially the framework above at least allows us to group measures according to the relevant stage in the process.

Developing Impact Measures

So what outcome impacts should we be measuring? Traditional recruitment and retention metrics should certainly be part of the picture. But most commentators now agree that the effects of employer branding are potentially much more far-reaching. Some start by arguing that there is a straightforward link from improvement in recruitment and engagement performance to bottom-line profit, and that measures such as value added per employee or even net income per employee are valid metrics for employer branding. Others stop short of this, but include more focused financial measures such as overall compensation and benefits costs, recruitment costs, time lost through absence and so on.

There is more fundamental agreement about other consequences, though. Most HR and marketing professionals agree that there is a direct link from employee engagement through the service-profit chain to improved customer satisfaction, customer loyalty and profit, and that this is important to measure. And it's not just the level of satisfaction that's important; it's also the nature of the interaction: in particular, the delivery of overall 'one-brand' values. The way in which employees behave in delivering customer service – in 'living the brand' – will impact significantly on perceptions of the consumer brand.

Jenny Strevens shows in the case study included in this chapter how the RBS Group measures its employer brand strength. But this is part of a much wider human capital management strategy that includes a wide range of metrics to monitor the financial impacts of HR and branding activities. This work has revealed many examples both of correlations between employee engagement and customer satisfaction and of the significant cost savings that engagement improvements can bring. For example a 1 per cent decrease in staff turnover saved the business £30 million a year and a 0.2 per cent decrease in absence saved it a further £6 million.[2]

Another measure shows a 10 per cent increase in leadership effectiveness driving a 3 per cent increase in customer satisfaction. However, as Greg Aitken, head of human capital strategy at RBS, points out, what matters most – more than immediate financial returns – is 'creating strategic advantage' through delivering a customer experience that enhances its consumer brand position.[3]

A company's reputation as an employer will also affect how it is seen in the wider business and financial community in terms of its success and quality of management. The economist Bryan Finn, at Business Economics, has developed econometric models to show how 'the ability to attract, develop and retain top talent' helps drive a company's 'non-financial reputation', which in turns helps drive overall corporate reputation, which is a key driver of market capitalisation.[4] So, if you want to, you can track your employer branding efforts all the way through from advertising expenditure to stock market valuation.

The key point here comes back to our 'one-brand' argument in Chapter 2 and discussion of engagement in Chapter 3. Everything that an organisation does through employer branding programmes is part of a much bigger picture and will inevitably have consequences for other facets of the overall master brand.

Figure 11.2 shows a potential 'scorecard' approach to impact metrics.

Potential Impact Metrics

We don't want to be prescriptive in this book, believing instead that individual organisations are best placed to determine which measures they should use. We have highlighted some of the main aspects that we believe are important to

---

2   *Financial Times*, 18 April 2007 at: http://www.ft.com/cms/s/0/31eb3250-ed95-11db-8584-000b5df10621.html.
3   Greg Aitken, 'RBS: Using People Intelligence to Improve Performance', *Journal of Applied Human Capital Management*, 1(2), 2007, pp. 81–84.
4   Bryan Finn, 'Modelling the Drivers of Corporate Reputation and its Connection with Shareholder Value', unpublished document, Business Economics Ltd, 2007.

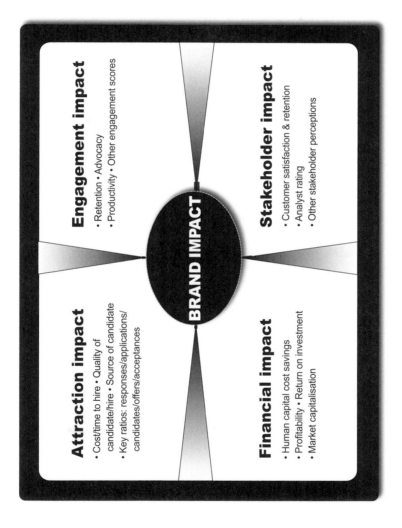

Figure 11.2   Measuring employer brand impact

measure against each area of impact in the model depicted in Figure 11.2, and others are shown below. We discuss some of the issues relating to definition and choice of exact measures later in this chapter.

RECRUITMENT IMPACT

- Quantity of expressions of interest;

- Quantity of applications – from *suitable* candidates;

- Source of candidates (all channels, especially percentage sourced directly/unsolicited);

- Referrals received from existing employees;

- Quality of candidates – versus set thresholds (CV screening and so on);

- Demographics of candidates (diversity versus existing workforce);

- Candidates lost during recruitment process;

- Key ratios: interest/applicants/candidates/offers/acceptance;

- Quality of hires versus set criteria;

- Hiring manager satisfaction;

- Vacancies filled (including 'difficult to fill' vacancies);

- Cost of hiring/filling a vacancy (but note the discussion of more sophisticated measures later);

- Time to hire/fill vacancy/for employee to start;

- New hire performance & productivity.

ENGAGEMENT IMPACT

- Turnover/retention rates;

- by all demographics/tenure;

- Cost of leavers;

- Cost of unfilled vacancies;

- Key productivity and performance measures;

- Rate of staff suggestions;

- Referral levels;

- Sickness absence levels.

CONSUMER IMPACT

- Consumer satisfaction (with service levels);

- Consumers feeling that staff live the brand.

FINANCIAL IMPACT

- Recruitment process costs (advertising, agency fees, management interviewing time, assessment centres);

- Turnover costs (redundancy, re-recruitment costs);

- Human capital costs (total payroll, pay per grade, absence costs, 'shrinkage' costs);

- Productivity/output (added value per employee);

- Profitability (net profit per employee);

- Share price/market capitalisation;

- Return on investment.

Pre-empting our discussion of measurement issues later, we emphasise that these are only *potential* measures and that we are not recommending adoption of all of them. Organisations need to differentiate between 'need to have' and 'nice to have'.

Return on Investment

Returning to the question of evaluation, calculating the impacts on an organisation is, of course, only half of the answer to the question 'Is it worth it?' To assess return on investment, and continually monitor the efficiency of the employer branding process, we need to keep a firm track of the investment going in: the inputs and associated outputs. As with impact metrics, at the moment this does not happen universally. Indeed, the recent CIPD *Recruitment, Retention and Turnover* survey[5] found that only 51 per cent of respondents said that they calculated recruitment costs.

INPUTS

Some of the inputs, being largely financial, are in fact mentioned above as potential impacts in their own right – recruitment costs are one input into the employer branding process that could decrease as a result of good brand performance. Others are more time-based, but equally quantifiable, and all should be monitored and recorded:

INPUTS

- Total expenditure by all branding activities;

- Recruitment/engagement teams/ FTE posts;

- Other time inputs – for example, management time spent interviewing.

OUTPUTS

All outputs from the process – what the money is being spent on – could be similarly recorded. There are advantages in doing this, as it provides background information for evaluation. However, the danger then arises of measuring for measurement's sake, and it would be sensible to choose only a few key metrics that represent major outputs, such as:

- Communications outputs;

---

5   CIPD, *Recruitment, Retention and Turnover*, Annual Survey Report 2008. Available at: http://www.cipd.co.uk/NR/rdonlyres/BE3C57BF-91FF-4AD0-9656-FAC27E5398AA/0/ recruitmentretentionturnover2008.pdf.

- Advertisements, articles published;

- Readership of advertisements/articles;

- Internal communications outputs;

- Website/intranet visits;

- Candidate packs produced;

- Workshops run;

- Leadership/behavioural programmes run;

- Surveys conducted;

- Adherence of all activities to brand guidelines.

Monitoring the *Process* of Employer Brand Management

As well as measuring impact, the other key use for metrics is to assess and gauge the success of the branding *process*.

Your strategy for developing your employer brand should include asking 'How, exactly, are we trying to do this, and what effect is all this having?' To be successful, you should develop a model which shows the intended consequences of your actions (in terms of the outputs described above) and, especially, how you are attempting to influence perceptions of your employer brand and consequent changes in attitudes and intentions among current and potential employees. Even before this, of course, you need to be clear about exactly what an employer brand is to your organisation – what its components are and your vision, or targets, for each one.

In Chapters 2 and 3 we explained our suggested approach to defining and managing an employer brand. We talked about employer brands as comprising a number of attributes, including benefits, values and personalities, and as aiming to make organisations attractive and distinctive as employers. We mentioned propositions, 'deals' and experiences across the employee lifecycle.

And we stressed the need for segmentation in defining sub-EVPs to appeal to different groups.

All of these need defining and continual monitoring through a robust set of metrics as part of the implementation process.

Developing Process Metrics

Initially, the key process objective of employer branding is to manage the brand image that exists in the minds of your current and potential employees. More specifically, it is to bring this 'current brand image' closer to the vision you have for the brand, developed using the processes described in Chapter 2.

The first task, therefore, is to monitor the extent to which this is happening. Figure 11.3 represents on example – often found – of partial overlap between current brand image and brand vision. If the key to employer branding is to bring these further images together, we need to measure and constantly monitor the gap. To do this, we first need to define the agreed components of an employer brand image and the values you would like it to take on. This is discussed in Chapter 3, but we repeat the model here for clarity (see Figure 11.4).

Whichever attributes you choose for your brand vision, you will need to know, first, whether perceptions of the brand among current and potential

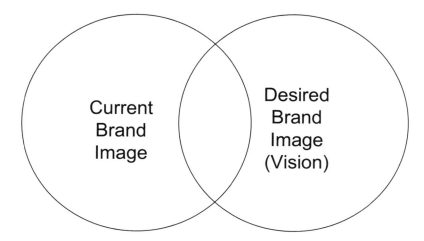

Figure 11.3   **Current versus desired employer brand image**

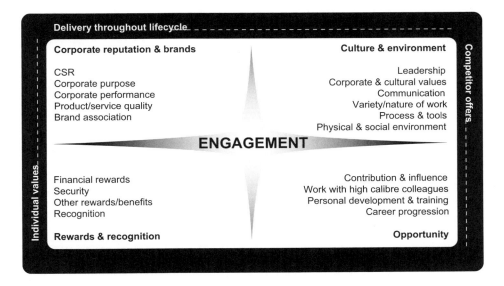

Figure 11.4   Key components of employee engagement

employees match these and, second, what this means in terms of likely behaviour.

So, for example, Marks and Spencer's ten-point promise that Keith Cameron described in Chapter 5 could be seen as their brand vision – the company wants to be known for offering this package of benefits. The extent to which the brand *image* overlaps with this will depend on: a) their actual performance in delivering the promise; and b) how this is communicated internally and externally. Both can be measured through qualitative or, more likely, quantitative research.

The second part to the process metrics story is the 'so what' part. Changes in *perceptions* are all very well, but it's changes in *attitude* that are more important – with 'attitude' used in its proper sense, implicitly carrying some indication of a disposition or tendency to do something: in this case either to apply for a job or to stay and engage with you as an employer.

The link between perceptions and attitudes depends on a number of factors, the most important of which are:

- the value attached to each attribute in relation to individual desires and motivations;

- the degree of the promise's credibility;

- how differentiating the offer is compared with competitors' brand offerings.

It is useful to remind ourselves here of the two sides to the EVP: the 'price' to be paid by the employee is just as important as the benefits on offer (see Figure 11.5).

Regular monitoring of all of these perceptions and attitudes, if done properly, allows employers to adjust the brand vision and its delivery and communication as necessary. For example, if the metrics show that your brand vision is believed both internally and externally, but that what you offer simply isn't valued by large sections of your target market or that all your competitors are positioning themselves in the same way, then it's time to redefine the brand vision.

This is one of the reasons for conducting specific brand research programmes alongside more orthodox employee survey work. At Bernard Hodes Group, we are often asked by clients if, in developing and monitoring an employer brand,

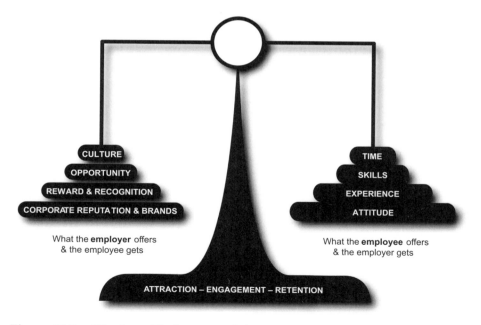

Figure 11.5   The brand balance model

we can use the outputs from 'standard' employee engagement questionnaire surveys. Whilst these surveys will undoubtedly cover many of the topics described above, they usually only ask employees about current levels of satisfaction in absolute terms, with no reference to what this 'satisfaction' means – whether the attribute in question is important to someone or whether it is delivered any differently there than in any other organisation. Defining and adjusting employer brands requires a different level of insight, going beyond the obvious 'Are you proud to work for company x?' Our question is always: 'why?'

There are certain points along the employee lifecycle where specific questions need to be asked – of candidates, new hires and leavers, for example. These are the groups where changes in perceptions are playing out in live actions – in joining or leaving the organisation – and are thus especially valuable to understand.

Potential Process Metrics

INTERNALLY – CURRENT EMPLOYEES

- Perceptions of desired brand attributes:

  - attractive,

  - credible,

  - differentiating.

- Perceptions of competitors on same criteria;

- Brand promises being kept;

- Key engagement scores:

  - pride in working for you,

  - intentions to leave,

  - propensity to recommend.

- Reasons for leaving;

- Externally – potential employees;

- Awareness of you as an employer;

- Perceptions of desired brand attributes:

    - attractive,

    - credible,

    - differentiating,

- Perceptions of competitors on same criteria;

- Willingness to consider you as an employer;

- Position as 'ideal employer' by target segment (for example, on ST Top 100);

- Candidate perceptions/satisfaction.

From What to How: Some Questions of Measurement

We have discussed the potential scope of the measurement exercise relating to employer branding and suggested some possible metrics. But which approach is right for you? Incorporating metrics into an employer brand development programme sounds eminently sensible, so why isn't everyone doing it?

Adopting metrics, of course, has significant implications. It's not free; it's not even cheap – gathering information to the required level of detail can be very costly. It may be tempting to use existing information sources such as routine employee surveys as much as possible – but does this give you what you need? And if you need to choose new measures, which ones are best for you, and when is the best time to measure? We discuss some of these questions on the following pages.

THE COST OF MEASURING

We've established that you need to monitor the cost of employer branding, but what about the cost of monitoring itself? This is probably largely a question of time – whoever takes responsibility for this activity could potentially need to gather, store and analyse a great deal of data. This would inevitably include time spent chasing not only HR colleagues, but also departmental managers responsible for hiring and related expenditure. There may also be financial implications in developing new systems or employing research consultants, and employers should be aware of these costs from the outset.

WHAT TO MEASURE

The first question is the breadth and depth of measurement you are willing or able to commit to in this exercise. As we have noted, measurement is time-consuming and potentially expensive, so unless it's in your organisation's culture to measure everything that moves (and some do), it may be better to focus – at least initially – on what is achievable and unquestionably useful.

Whatever the culture of your organisation, you need to adopt some guiding principles regarding metrics that will guide you in defining measures. The approach to metrics adopted by different organisations is regularly featured in the HR press, and in researching this book we have come across many different ideologies.

The principle at Philips, for example, is to 'focus the team on a few selected goals, and to celebrate successes when you hit a target and are moving in the right direction'.[6] Philips has built a system around three key measures of employer brand strength, monitoring whether potential employees in different groups:

- are familiar with the company;

- would consider Philips as an employer;

- rank Philips as their ideal employer.

On the other hand, there are examples of large, often US, corporations (and increasingly specialist consulting firms) who adopt tens or hundreds of measures to cover everything from the number of application packs sent out to change in value added per employee.

---

6   CIPD, *Employer Branding, op. cit.*

Which approach is right for you? One principle may be to fit the choice of metrics to your current business goals. A recent article published by Staffing.org, the US recruitment metrics consultants, highlighted different scenarios where companies at different stages in their growth needed different HR metrics.[7] For example, where a company is expanding rapidly in certain markets, time to hire (and time to competency) will be critical. Where longer-term growth plans are more important, quality of hire is a better measure.

It's certainly true that adopting a wide range of HR process metrics will help to ensure that recruitment and retention processes are run efficiently, and that short-term tactical goal fulfilment can be measured. But we'd like to suggest that most effort in developing *branding* impact metrics should be put into measuring longer-term impacts on the strategic ability of an organisation to recruit and retain talent. So quality of hire and retention and engagement of high performers should be priority measures, along with some measure of impact on other aspects of the consumer/corporate brand.

What Do Metrics Really Tell You?

What you decide to measure may depend not only on the potential costs of information gathering, but also on how useful you feel certain metrics really are. There are certainly some who will feel that getting the right quality of information necessary to produce meaningful and useful statistics across more than, say, 10–20 measures would be disproportionate.

The usefulness of metrics will depend on several factors, including how they are defined and the accuracy of the data used to support them. A sensible approach would be to only choose measures which you feel can be easily implemented and which will have some concrete use in the branding process.

As an example, the usefulness of the typical 'cost per hire' metric – relatively easy to collect, you might think – has long been questioned, not least because decreasing cost doesn't necessarily lead to the best outcome (increasing costs may in fact bring better candidates). Many have argued that 'quality of hire' is a much more useful measure. But does the quality of data available to enable assessment of this measure support its use?

---

7   David Earle, 'Which Metrics Are You Talking About?', Staffing.org, 10 March 2007 at: http://
     www.staffing.org/library_ViewArticle.asp?ArticleID=324,

Some of our colleagues from Bernard Hodes Group in the US have argued that quality of hire is so difficult to pin down that its use is limited. Some organisations attempt to measure quality by monitoring how satisfied hiring managers are with their new recruits, but there is an inherent bias in this measure: in doing this, hiring managers are effectively rating their own performance as recruiters and thus tend to be too positive. The answer may be to focus on measuring quality of *applicant* instead: raising this should automatically mean better hires, and it is far easier to measure at various points in the recruitment process (for example, the prevalence of required *qualifications*, assessed through CV screening).

Other industry experts such as Staffing.org have put forward alternative measures to cost-per-hire, such as recruiting cost ratio and recruiting efficiency ratio. These relate costs of recruiting (both the cost of new employees in terms of their salaries and the cost of the recruitment process itself) to the relevant total costs for the organisation.

Time-to-hire is another controversial metric – fastest isn't always best, as companies like Google and Goldman Sachs will tell you. Other companies are only concerned that their calculated hiring times are not exceeded, not that this should be reduced at the expense of quality hires.

All these examples highlight the care that should be taken when selecting the best measures for you. Rather than be overprescriptive here, we simply suggest that you look carefully at the range of measures available, choose a cross-section of process and impact measures, and debate internally which would be most useful and sensible for you.

Finally, we should stress that it's also important to choose a balance of measures to look at the entire employee lifecycle, not just recruitment. Here, too, there are issues around measurement.

When assessing perceptions and attitudes, great care needs to be taken in ensuring accuracy. But do companies always use appropriate research methodology with care? Many companies conduct their own exit interviews, for example, and attempt to identify key reasons – push and pull factors – why people leave. It is commonly thought by HR professionals that individual managers are a key reason for many people leaving an employer. But this is not always picked up in internal exit interviews, with leavers sometimes reluctant to blame their bosses in front of a colleague, or because the manager had successfully passed the blame on to the organisation in the mind of the employee. This is one reason why we believe exit interviewing, along with many other aspects of the metrics process, is best done by independent consultants, skilled in understanding what people are really telling you.

Benchmarking

The measurement process can be enhanced if you can find useful external benchmarks to compare your findings with. Some consultancy firms will be able – at a cost – to supply these, but there are also public sources available. For example, the 2008 CIPD *Recruitment, Retention and Turnover* survey reports that the average cost of filling a vacancy is 'currently £4,667, increasing to £5,800 when organisations are also calculating the associated labour turnover costs'.[8] The median labour turnover rate amongst respondents was 17.3 per cent

The caveats and qualifications mentioned here remind us that if you want to benchmark, you need to ensure that the definition of your metrics matches the benchmark definitions. Organisations may well decide that being able to define metrics according to their own specific needs is more useful than being able to compare with other, less useful measures.

The other pitfall of benchmarks is that averages vary significantly between sectors and types of organisation. As an example, the latest Staffing.org benchmark report found that, amongst its American respondents:

- *There is wide variation in Cost-Per-Hire from industry to industry, with Retailing and Hospitality at the low end (approximately $2,000) and Pharma Biotech on the high end at more than $16,000.*

- *Time-To-Start averages 7–8 weeks across all industries, with a one-week discrepancy between promise and performance. Larger companies report longer average hiring times, but with a smaller discrepancy. Again, there are substantial differences between industry groups (from Retailing at about four weeks to Government at about 12).*[9]

---

8   CIPD, *Recruitment, Retention and Turnover, op. cit.,* p. 2.
9   'Benchmark Report, Executive Summary', Staffing.org, 6 November 2008 at: http://staffing.org/ library_ViewArticle.asp?ArticleID=384.

The benchmark supplier must therefore be able to provide a large enough subsample to enable meaningful comparisons. This is not always possible.

The Issue of Causality

The issue of causality is a significant one. Previously, we've talked about employer branding communication and other activities 'leading to' changes in perceptions and attitudes, which 'cause' changes (hopefully improvements) in recruitment and retention performance. But does this logic reflect reality?

This is not an academic issue. It matters because it is at the heart of assessing the efficiency and effectiveness of what we are all trying to do. This is recognised in major advertising awards (where, for some reason, 'effectiveness' is still often in a special category).

As Hertfordshire Constabulary found out when putting itself forward for the IPA Effectiveness Awards in 2004,[10] identifying causality is not straightforward. However, by careful correlation of various metrics, including advertising activity and spend, the number of enquiries and applications received through dedicated channels and the number of recruits per intake, Hertfordshire calculated that it had made major cost savings and significantly improved gender ratios. Interestingly, the Constabulary demonstrated that, without their employer branding campaign, it could only have achieved a similar result in increasing application levels by equalising their salary levels with the neighbouring Metropolitan Police Force. This would have cost some £12 million. So, clearly, the gap between this and the cost of employer branding can justifiably be counted as a major impact.

When to Measure

Measurement should really be an ongoing process, with systems set up to record inputs and outputs as they happen. We suggest that most of the ultimate impact measures discussed above should also be monitored regularly. The ones based on financial data, in particular, should be readily available, and most large employers should now have applicant tracking and recruitment systems that should provide good quality HR data. Together with consumer brand data

---

10 'Police Officer Recruitment', Chapter 15 in *Advertising Works 13*, WARC, Henley-on-Thames, 2005.

from your marketing department, these should probably be reviewed at least quarterly, and certainly biannually.

This is also probably true of process measures: quarterly tracking and review would be ideal, but possibly beyond the resources of all but the largest organisations. Annual frameworks already exist for many employers in the form of regular engagement surveys or participation in such competitions as *The Sunday Times* Top 100 Employers. We would suggest that an annual review of brand perceptions may miss subtle changes in attitudes or market conditions and that more frequent monitoring may allow you to stay one step ahead of the competition. Best practice in this area is probably a regular or continuous programme of surveys and focus groups that keep you in touch with employee opinion. Internal 'pulse' surveys of this kind are becoming increasing popular. This approach could also be applied externally in monitoring the pulse of potential employee opinion.

Finally, perhaps more important than how frequently you monitor your brand position is what you do with the information. As we said at the start of this chapter, although evaluating employer branding could be seen as coming at the 'end' of the process, in fact it is really only a 'feedback' stage which should be used to adjust inputs, outputs and intended outcomes for the next round. The measurement cycle then starts all over again.

Building the Business Case

Hopefully, this overview of metrics has given an idea of what measures you could use in implementing an employer brand programme and measuring its success. There is one final area to discuss, however. What's the best way of selling the idea of employer branding to budget-holders and decision-makers inside the organisation in the first place?

The fact that you are prepared to monitor inputs, outputs, outcomes and impacts is likely to help you with this: securing funding is much easier if internal investors can see that it will be properly spent. As we said at the start, 'What is this exercise going to do for us?' and 'How can we measure its impact?' are the questions that internal powers will ask.

Ultimately, it may be the adoption of key measures as targets that swings the balance. Projecting target increases in productivity and profitability as a result of employer branding may not be feasible, but suggesting to your board that recruitment costs are likely to decrease and key engagement measures improve is certainly not unrealistic. This may involve taking the key measures you have decided to adopt and tracking back to measure what has actually happened in the last few years. The question then becomes: 'What will happen if we decide *not* to actively manage our employer brand?'

Again, the choice of which targets to adopt will depend on your organisation's culture, but it would be wise to consider formulating at least a view on the likely nature of the return on investment to help build your case for employer branding.

CASE STUDY – ROYAL BANK OF SCOTLAND

Jenny Strevens

The Royal Bank of Scotland Group (RBS) has a global reach in over 50 countries worldwide, serving over 40 million customers. Founded in 1727, the group has around 170,000 employees – having grown from 30,000 employees in ten years. RBS's brands include RBS, NatWest, Coutts, Ulster Bank, Direct Line, Tesco Personal Finance and Citizens Bank. They are the No. 1 corporate bank in the UK and Europe and No. 5 in the US and Asia Pacific (excluding Japan).

To recruit and retain the best talent for RBS in all our target markets it is critical to have a distinctive and completing employer brand.[1]

As it is vital to demonstrate the true value of our employer brand and build the credibility of this work across the business, we need to have the ability to measure it. Within the RBS group, we have developed metrics which demonstrates that our measure of employer brand is highly correlated with both sales and customer service results. In fact, this has shown that the correlation between these measures and employer brand is stronger than the correlation to employee engagement. As a result, our employer brand index is another credible measure within the service-profit chain.

To enable us to measure our employer brand index, we had to articulate what our employer brand is in terms of the proposition for potential and existing employees. This is the first vital step towards being able to measure it. We achieved this through extensive internal and external research. This established the perceptions of RBS which we matched to the spirit of Make it Happen™ (our global strap-line).

We were able to identify four themes or pillars of our employer brand and an

---

1   Susan Bor, Director Group Resourcing, RBS Group.

overarching principle of working together. These are the four things that underpin our ability to Make it Happen™. To explain these further, they are the foundations of what make RBS a great place to work; they are proven to be true of the Group and are valued by our employees. Importantly they contribute to our successful performance as a business and make us different from the competition.

The four pillars are:

1. *Power to perform* – our ability to provide excellent service to our customers and deliver results

2. *Opportunity to grow* – our dynamic environment which creates opportunities to share ideas and learn from colleagues, as well as the potential to move into new areas and pursue a number of different career paths

3. *Responsive to your needs* – recognising that our success is a result of our people being motivated, open-minded and actively contributing to new ideas, and encouraging our people to lead a healthy work–life balance.

4. *Ambition to succeed* – we have achieved our growth and success by setting our sights high, staying focused and celebrating success. We seek to employ talented people who have a winning team spirit and enjoy the challenge of going one better.

The glue for these four pillars is our overarching principle of working together. This involves our people working with each other to achieve results for customers and therefore business success.

We were then able to determine a measure of our employer brand proposition by incorporating this into the global employee opinion survey – 'Your Feedback'. This survey is sent to every employee in the group, resulting in 129,000 responses in 2007 (90 per cent). A core set of questions are asked, and from this set we identified specific questions which represented the four pillars and the overall principle. By using the percentage of favourable responses to these questions, we were able to create a core employer brand index and examine the perceptions of the components which make it up. Due to the extensive and thorough coverage of the survey, the employer brand index can be identified across multiple demographics including business unit, position in the group, working patterns, age, gender and geography.

A summary of our 2007 results by geographic region is shown in Table 11.1.

From Table 11.1 you can see that the further away from the corporate headquarters, the lower the employer brand index. This finding confirms that having a local/ regional focus is critical to building a strong employer brand elsewhere in the Group's emerging markets, where the RBS corporate brand is less well known.

So by using our in-depth annual employee opinion survey, we can obtain the updated position for our employer brand performance and supplement that with

Table 11.1   Feedback survey: summary of results, 2007

Component	Difference from RBS group score		
	Europe & Middle East	North America	Asia
Employer brand index	1	-3	-4
Working together	1	-2	-3
Ambition to succeed	1	-3	-3
Responsive to your needs	1	-4	-1
Power to perform	1	-2	-5
Opportunity to grow	1	-3	-4

the continual external (and largely qualitative) research that we conduct in our new and core geographies. Benchmarking is something which we view as key to our human capital model as it allows us to put our results in context – for example, when measuring employee engagement there are consistent measures used across organisations, cultures and geographies that allow benchmarks to be set. The same is not true for employer branding – and nor should it be. As our employer brand index measures what Make it Happen™ means and how it is being delivered, this is not comparable to other organisations. Therefore we have no external benchmark, but our internal benchmark is to ensure that we have a strong employer brand across all geographies, employee segments and businesses. The information we have collated to date tells us that there are differences, but that these are relatively small variances. This means that we can demonstrate through metrics that we have a strong platform to build upon to ensure that we continue to deliver and build upon the Make it Happen™ employer brand promises.

12

The Future – Where Next for Employer Brands?

Helen Rosethorn
Bernard Hodes Group

In this book, we have charted the course of the concept of the employer brand, examining its origins and looking at how you might start to define and manage it. We have also understood in more detail the deal that lies at the heart of it and how that is evolving across the global stage.

We have tested how the concept plays out in the working lives of five very different organisations. Some of these companies use the idea of the employer brand explicitly; others acknowledge the concept more implicitly through the way in which they consider the expectations of the contract between themselves and their people.

We have also examined the practical question of ownership. If an organisation is to define and manage this deal, should someone be ultimately accountable for its delivery or is this responsibility shared amongst key stakeholders? Similarly, we have explored the question of measurement – building the case for beginning an employer branding journey demands a view of return on investment and begs the question of exactly how you assess the value of this concept.

Now it's time to look towards the future. Assuming you buy into the core of this idea and can appreciate the value it adds to organisational thinking today, it's important to ask where it will take proponents and practitioners tomorrow.

Brands that endure are seen to be relevant through changing times. It is, of course, fair to say that brands come and go. However, the ones that stand the test of time do so because they continue to offer us, the consumers, a deal that we see as relevant, despite changing wants, needs and circumstances.

For any employer brand to endure it must, of course, do the same. So what changes do employers and their brands need to be aware of? What is coming over the horizon to challenge employer brands in their quest for relevance and meaning to their consumers?

We see four key changes and issues that employer brands need to respond to. These changes are not simple workplace issues, but are more socioeconomic or geopolitical in their nature and reach, although employers will need to translate these into meaning in the workplace where so many of us spend most of our time. Only by doing this will brands retain their relevance and meaning for us.

The four key changes employers must consider are:

1.   shifting value systems and brands with a conscience;

2.   the digital world and brands in cyberspace;

3.   a new world order;

4.   our need to belong.

Shifting Value Systems

In Chapter 1 we talked about changing views on loyalty and what the purpose of the organisation should be. There has never been a heyday when corporations acted for the benefit of society or the environment. However, with the unprecedented power of business – public and private – in recent decades and the emergence of a more informed and educated population, the debate around what an organisation stands for has been intensified.

The phrase 'corporate social responsibility' (CSR) was first tabled in 1953 with the publication of Howard Bowen's *Social Responsibilities of the Businessman*.[1] This posed the question: 'What responsibilities to society can business people be reasonably expected to assume?'

---

1   Howard Bowen, *Social Responsibilities of the Businessman*, Harper & Row, New York, 1953.

Throughout the 1970s and 1980s, academic discussion of the concept of CSR intensified, but many would judge that CSR has only grown in importance as organisations have sought to fight back after public scandals and mismanagement. Turning-points are seen as Shell's problems in 1995 with Nigeria and Brent Spar and, more recently, the collapse of Enron in 2001. But there have been other spurs to activity which have not simply been about corporate PR crises. We have all become concerned about issues like global warming thanks to the missionary zeal of people like Al Gore and his movie, *An Inconvenient Truth*, in 2006.

These are the catalysts to a different value system now at play, which is close to the hearts of consumers of many different goods and services, including consumers of jobs. Evidence of this is now emerging, one example being research findings published by our Omnicom sister company Fleishman-Hillard in May 2007 in conjunction with The National Consumer League.[2] The research was limited to the US, but it asked consumers an interesting question –what did they consider the most important CSR issue for organisations today? Treating and rewarding employees well was the top answer by some considerable margin (see Figure 12.1).

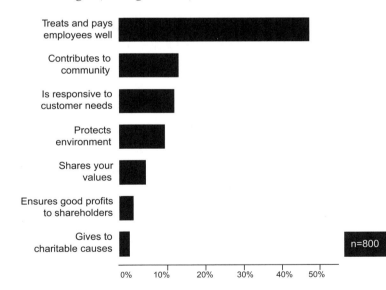

Figure 12.1   The most important CSR issue

2   'Rethinking Corporate Social Responsibility: A Fleishman-Hillard/National Consumer League Study', White Paper, May 2007 at: http://www.fleishman.com/point-of-view/docs/csr_white_paper.pdf.

This answer was further validated in the survey by answers to the question 'What is the meaning of CSR?' 'Commitment to employees' came in top at 27 per cent of respondents, with 'commitment to communities' coming second at 23 per cent.

The obvious and direct link between the employees of an organisation and the communities which it serves and from which it also likely to draw its people is the basis of the concept of diversity. In the 1990s this notion catapulted onto the business agenda in the US and Western Europe. Its early proponents rarely defined it in relation to CSR, although it can be helpful to see diversity as a subset of social responsibility. What's more, the early drivers of the notion were not always egalitarian, and the first definitions of diversity were often quite primitive. So, for example, there were legislative pressures to meet quotas for minority representation in the US and in the UK certain public-sector organisations also took up targets, some passed down by government.

At the same time, marketing departments discovered the benefits of audience mirroring. They began suggesting that to be more appealing to the increasingly varied customer base served in cosmopolitan Western societies, employees had to be more of a reflection of the customers they served. Put simply, a more representative workforce would produce a more engaging customer experience.

However, more organisations have come to challenge these early approaches, suggesting that diversity is better served by developing an inclusive organisational environment. The focus then becomes the multiple dimensions to diversity, rather than the classic issues concerning representation and discrimination on the basis of ethnic origin, gender, age, religious and sexual orientation. The important point here is that increasingly good practice with regard to being a diverse, if not inclusive, employer is seen as part of CSR. Indeed, diversity is almost a mandatory factor within CSR, and is indicative of what an organisation stands for.

Even though we look at a brand from different perspectives, depending on whether we are a consumer, shareholder, supplier or employee (remember our model from Chapter 1) a sense of shared values was emerging as important on all dimensions (see Figure 12.2).

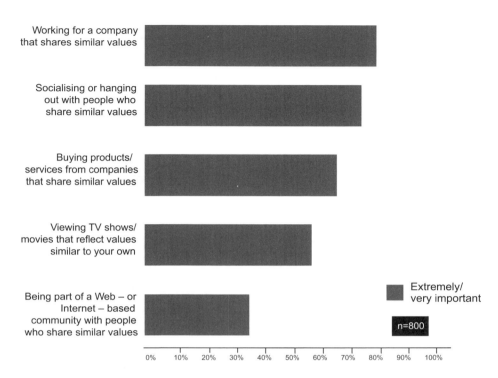

Figure 12.2   Values, moral principles and ethics

A final result of interest from this research concerned how consumers form their views. They believe less and less in what they hear from traditional media sources and 'those in authority' and make their decision based on what they glean from their own networks and experiences.

So what is this telling us about employer brands and the link to CSR? In short, the dynamic between the two counts more than ever before. And, even more importantly, one feeds the other. As consumers, we expect and demand the corporations behind well-known brands to be good employers. Therefore, with a reputation as a good employer, a corporation can drive value to the bottom line. You cannot build a sustainable employer reputation if you are not aligned with the value systems of today, and CSR is the greatest test.

Brands with a Conscience

So which brands are taking advantage of the dynamic between CSR, employee reputation and engagement and how is it working for them?

The 'early adopters' were those that linked employee volunteering and the 'giving' agenda of the organisation – such as Nokia and their world-renowned 'Helping Hands' programme. It soon became clear, though, that the payback from schemes like this had great potential. HSBC has an impressive record of donating to major environmental charities and involving its employees – but the organisation did not anticipate the impact on its employee engagement when it first donated $50 million to three environmental charities in 2002.[3] HSBC involved the University of Cambridge Programme for Industry (CIP) to look at what exactly was happening. CIP reported: 'people were given a profound experience; they could really see the importance of it, could engage in a new way, and feel proud that they worked for such an organisation'.

Let us return to the question of treating and rewarding employees well. The reward issue is an interesting one. Research carried out by TSC late in 2007 demonstrated that people would potentially compromise their salary to work for a company with a good CSR policy.[4] We are aware of research done inside a major global bank which has also supported this finding.

Whilst the reward issue is an emotive one, many public-sector organisations have indeed found over the years that they are able to attract and keep talent in the face of fierce competition because people join and stay 'to make a difference'. The L&Q Group picks up on this point in its case study (see Chapter 8).

More often, organisations are aiming to demonstrate their commitment to employees on the wider 'well-being' agenda – supporting the health and welfare of their people and going beyond the simple reward 'benefit' of private healthcare. Of course, in many nations this is clearly good business sense, given some of the health issues playing out in working life.

In the UK, the Department of Health attributes the loss of up to 18 million working days per year to obesity-related illness, whilst the HSE calculates that 113.8 million working days were lost to stress, depression or anxiety-related ill-health in 2006–07.[5] There are fears that, with a direct correlation between debt worries and stress, these numbers will be even higher in 2008 due to the effects of the 'credit crunch'.[6]

---

3   Tim Smedley, 'A Little More Conservation', *People Management* 11 January 2007.
4   Sue Harrington, 'CSR Research: Make a Difference', *HR Magazine*, 4 January 2008. Available at: http://www.humanresourcesmagazine.com/news/774913.
5   Simon Kent, 'On Your Bike', *People Management* 21 February 2008.
6   Hashi Syedain, 'The Money Trap', *People Management* 10 January 2008.

Whether it is Proctor & Gamble's sleep pods for employees[7] or financial education programmes at GSK,[8] caring for the well-being of the workforce has become part of the deal on offer whilst recognising that there is a fine line between invading an individual's space and where an employer should rightfully tread. But some employers are not holding back, wrapping employee well-being into a wider commitment to taking CSR to a whole new level. A pioneer of this is Marks & Spencer – which has set the bar high with its Plan A programme. It has five pillars – one being health and the commitment to help thousands of customers and employees choose a healthier lifestyle.

There needs to be a note of caution for brands in the whole CSR arena, though. Most CSR agendas by their very nature cannot be delivered by the organisation working alone. Most organisations have to work with partners – typically charities and NGOs – or with other corporates adding weight to a particular cause – Bono's RED initiative being a classic example of this. At a time when the corporate brand is in ascendance and corporate reputation is being more carefully managed, charities are fighting to get their act together too. However, most charities, apart from those in the charity 'premier division' such as Oxfam and the Red Cross, are poor at brand management.

Co-branding is going to become ever more important – fine if your branding partner lives up to expectations, but dangerous if it does not. M&S has made a great statement about its employer brand by choosing to work with a global social change organisation called We Are What We Do. However, it's vital that the M&S brand follows through with that statement as it's now integral to their brand, too.

The Digital World and Brands in Cyberspace

The digitisation of media has revolutionised the relationship between consumers and brands by shifting the balance of power in consumers' favour. It has enabled people to do things, learn things, control their lives, access information, create, publish, communicate, when, where and how they choose.

In essence 'digital' has caused the world to revolve around the consumer; and it has impacted significantly on what brands must now do to continue to survive. Consumers are becoming more demanding, more exacting in their

---

7   *People Management* 14 June 2007, p. 14.
8   Syedain, 'The Money Trap', *op. cit.*

needs, more in control and more likely to become frustrated when they can't have their desire instantly satisfied. In being the catalyst for this change, digital is also best placed to address these heightened consumer expectations.

We often say that when a company goes online, it is stripping itself naked for the world to see. Disparities in communication, differences in the approach of related business units, even differences in the way in which agencies apply the brand value are openly available to see. In a world of mega-mergers and acquisitions, this has a huge impact on the way in which a prospect will engage with a brand.

From an organisational perspective, there may be perfectly rational explanations for the presentation of distinctly separate brand experiences. Parent companies may have distinctly different employer brands from their subdivisions and would want to ensure that a candidate's expectations are carefully and realistically managed from the start. However, from a candidate perspective, this experience can be incredibly confusing and offputting; it is like walking into a store, asking (what you perceive to be) a straightforward question and getting entirely different responses from two different employees.

The result of this has been recognition of the need to track and manage the candidate journey from the beginning to end. How often do we see a fantastic brand experience that is destroyed as soon as a candidate hits 'apply' or see beguiling campaigns that are completely disassociated from the look and feel of a corporate website? A campaign has to achieve a delicate balance between meeting the direct objectives of enticing prospects who are actively engaged in job-seeking to engage with the right client, whilst building up a level of engagements with target candidates who may not be considering moving at that particular point in time. In a world as exposed as the digital world, the failure to join up your communications says as much about your brand as any assessment centre or interview can deliver.

Today's job-seekers are no longer novices; they are familiar with a variety of online experiences. They know how and where to look for jobs, how to research companies, how to network and more. In other words, tired sites and outdated processes are not going to resonate with Web 2.0 candidates. Proprietary research[9] has indicated that candidates see an employer's website as an extension of the way in which they will be treated by the company that

---

9   '[A company's site] gives me an idea of what they think is important. (It is a) good way to judge
    the integrity and character of management, who approve the sites...'

they are researching. Many websites force a user to interpret their products and navigate through reams of different services, acronyms and terminologies; the whole experience can be confusing and depressing.

Why should this matter? In the face of uncertainty, users revert to things they know and trust. In the digital world, we are talking about their network. Whether or not you subscribe to the hype about Web 2.0 and beyond, it is clear that the rise of social networks is already starting to have a profound effect on the consumer–brand relationship. Organisations like Amazon understood this from the outset; with users posting comments, recommending books and self-regulating, suddenly the business model of book-trading shifted Amazon from being a processor of literature to a valued partner in the chain. What is powerful here is not the Amazon shopping application, but what Amazon does with the data that underlies it.

What does this mean for an employer brand? There are two key things to focus on: first, understand how people view your brand in an environment where potentially anything can be a communications medium and, second, in order to survive and grow, the brand relationship has to shift from a one-way transaction to a conversation.

Digital agencies have been swift to recognise this, and we are continually seeing campaigns where the brand has pushed the use of the channel to new extremes. Yell's award-winning 'Results for Real Life'[10] campaign in 2006 saw its search application taken to interactive six sheets at bus stops and GPS-enabled buses promoting local services; Nike[11] created an entire fitness programme where runners can buy GPS enabled shoes, linked to an iPod and not only track their performance on a bespoke microsite, but also download and share their favourite running tracks (see Figure 12.3).

Back in the 1990s NCR's Knowledge Lab[12] developed microwaves that doubled as voice-activated computers,[13] intelligent fridges that worked out your daily calorie count or ordered new food when stocks were declining, and watches that acted as wallets. The barrier between what can be imagined and

10 Internet Advertising Bureau Creative Showcase winner for 2006. See: http://www.creativeshowcase.net/en/1/thismonth.mxs?month=100601&pos=1.
11 http://nikeplus.nike.com/nikeplus/?locale=en_gb#humanraceredirect.
12 http://www.ncr.com. Also *What+if?*, the research journal of the NCR Knowledge Lab, Spring 1999, Autumn 1999, *Trends 2000*, various articles.
13 What+if?, the research journal of the NCR Knowledge Lab, Spring 1999, Autumn 1999, *Trends 2000*, various articles.

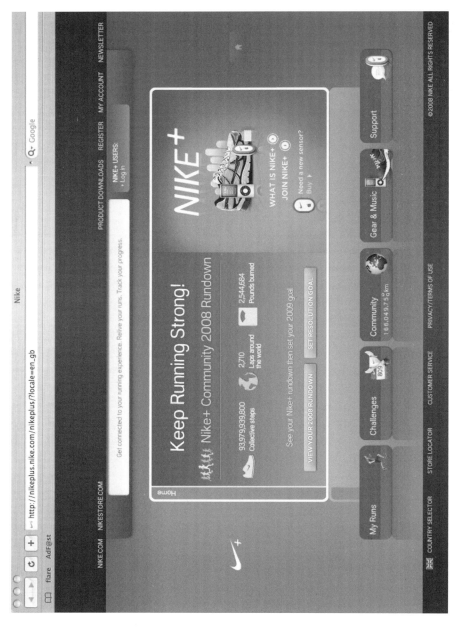

Figure 12.3   Nike and the Personal Trainer

what can be developed is now perilously thin, and anything has the potential to be a communications medium.

Figure 12.4 shows America's Army Online Recruitment Game, multi-media online role-playing game (MMORPG), developed by the US army, which gives prospective candidates an insight into the realities of army life.

Some employers are starting to recognise this change in the nature and consumer use of channel advertising and have been testing the impact of advertising in new channels: Yell, KMPG and RBS recently took part in a virtual careers fair[14] in Second Life; GCHQ purchased virtual billboard space in a range of games developed by Electronic Arts;[15] and the US army has developed a (popular) Internet military strategy game called America's Army[16] that doubles as a psychometric test.

In such a world there are very few brands that can afford to buy the advertising space to ensure that they are prevalent everywhere. But the paradox is that, in a world where the average consumer sees over a thousand adverts a day, brands need to be ever-present to ensure that they are heard. In the face of such adversity, intelligent brands are recognising the power of initiating conversations with prospective candidates.

Employee blogs sites, such as the HBOS Choices Graduate Blogs (see Figure 12.5), allow candidates to engage with a prospective employer on a more personal level.

Figure 12.6 shows the *Wall Street Journal* Careers Fair candidate lounge, providing a wealth of insight into the mind of the candidate pool.

In a summary of 2007, OnRec[17] described the year as the 'year of the blog'; if we look around at the majority of career websites, we see a plethora of blogs and vLogs, written (or ghost-written) by real employees to convey the reality of what it is like working at a specific company. The power of this simple message cannot be understated. Halifax,[18] for example, saw graduate applications

---

14 http://www.i-jobsforreal.co.uk.
15 http://www.guardian.co.uk/media/2007/oct/18/digitalmedia.advertising.
16 http://www.americasarmy.com.
17 Paula Santonocito, 'The Year in Online Recruitment', 15 January 2008 at: http://www.onrec. com/content2/news.asp?ID=19930.
18 'The HBOS Graduate Scheme, rated 55 in the 2008 *Times* Top 100 Employers Drives Traffic to a Bespoke Microsite' at: http://www.hbos-choices.co.uk.

Figure 12.4 America's Army Online Recruitment Game

HBOS plc

Home | Graduate schemes | Profiles | Blogs | Salary and benefits | About HBOS | HBOS culture | Learning and development | Events | FAQs | Application process

PREPARE to be amazed

WE'LL ENCOURAGE YOU TO EXPRESS YOURSELF.

BLOGS

At HBOS, we take pride in being an organisation where opinions count. From people in their first roles to those who are comfortable in the boardroom, everyone should be respected and listened to. That's why we've encouraged graduates on our schemes to write blogs about their experiences. It's an authentic look at the challenges they face and the support they receive. So, go ahead and have a read. It's a good opportunity to see what a career with us is like – straight from the horse's mouth.

Select a blog

Insight Investment
http://hbosinsightinvestment.blogspot.com

Treasury
http://hbostreasury.blogspot.com

Project Leaders
http://hbosretail.blogspot.com

Marketing
http://hbosretailmarketing.blogspot.com

Risk
http://hbosretailrisk.blogspot.com

Select a scheme

Salaries and benefits

Meet some Graduates

Apply online now

Training

We're committed to supporting you to achieve your goals. find out more

Graduate blogs

Our current graduates have been blogging their experiences. read them here

Figure 12.5   HBOS employee blog site

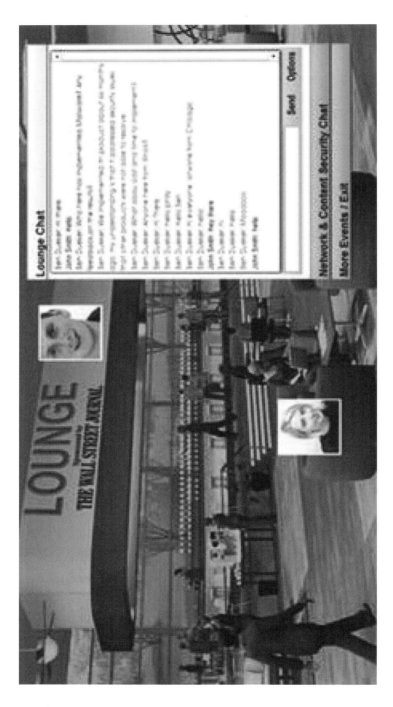

Figure 12.6   *Wall Street Journal* online careers fair

increase by over 50 per cent after introducing a blog[19] on their website, with over half of website users saying that they were 'more interested in HBOS' as a career prospect as a result of using the website.

However, it is not the blog per se but what the blog represents that is more important. Prospects want to not only read the information being presented to them, but also actively engage with it, deconstruct it and make it relevant to their personal needs.

Generation Y are experts at dissimilating reams of information, and therefore organisations have to go one step further and allow them to openly explore. At a recent *Wall Street Journal* virtual careers fair,[20] it was not the discussions in the employer booths, but the conversations that were taking place in the virtual lounge that were the most powerful. A more commonly seen example has been the rise of Facebook groups where current (and ex-) employees discuss brands, business units and even individuals to their hearts' content. (See 'Social Media Marketing' later in this chapter.)

A New World Order

Only two decades ago we were in a world dominated by Western economies – notably, of course, the US and Western Europe. Already that has changed, and this shift is set to continue until the 'West' no longer dominates. In time, it will sit alongside – if not be overtaken by – the Russian, Chinese and Indian economies, and this will have far-reaching consequences for employer brands.

As mentioned in Chapter 4, brands have historically travelled the globe in one particular trajectory – US- and European-originated corporations going 'multinational'. Some brands have taken this journey more successfully than others to become true global brands. They have been helped by the interest in brands as new developing nations like the former Soviet Union have emerged. In those countries, particularly Russia, the brands that became the most rapidly established were those which were aspirational – to do with modernity and Westernism. They might not have been the brands we would have chosen as symbols of the new world – more typically, they were fast-food and cigarette brands followed more recently by the most expensive car brands and top-end designer labels.

---

19 http://www.hbos-choices.co.uk/blogs/default.aspx.
20 http://www.wsj-classified.com/vcf/recruiter_showfloorgallery.html.

But this 'order' is changing. In the Western world we are already influenced more by brands from emerging and 'Eastern' economies than we potentially realise, and many organisations are having to think carefully about how they make their brands both global and local – 'glocalisation' as some would call it. In the past this may have simply meant 'cultural sensitivity', it demands much more now. Global is more global than ever before. And local is as granular as the individual; it involves reaching out and making that personal connection.

And in those more recently 'emerged' economies we now have brands going on their own global journeys – brands which will have to find their own way of 'glocalising' their propositions to brand audiences, whether customers, partners, shareholders or employees. This is another reason for the growing strength of the corporate brand in the architecture of brands – it has to offer a clearer roadmap and route to consistency. It is interesting to note that this is often the preferred branding architecture of many Asian organisations – many of which have been influencing the world order of brands for the last decade.

In future, employer brands need to travel the world, recognising that the balance of power has changed and that those brand propositions that were aspirational in the past do not necessarily reflect what will be aspirational in the future. If ever there were a case for the need to research and understand your audiences, this is it.

Our Need to Belong

We touched on the search for relationships when we referred to 'glocalisation' in the previous section. An employer brand has a big voice, if not *the voice*, on behalf of the organisation and employees, and potential employees need to feel that the voice is addressing them in a unique and individual, almost tailored, way. It seems that the more we become cynical about the voice of the organisation the more we fill the gap by investing our energies and engagement into our social networks.

Employer brands need to embrace this reality, and, although it most certainly can be to the organisation's advantage, many people worry that this is in conflict with allegiance to the employer brand. Some firms are putting blanket bans on Facebook and other social networking sites. However, this reveals a failure to appreciate the context of what is going on. You wouldn't ban employees from talking in a corridor, so why do it online? Whilst it is true that many of the conversations can be negative, it is also true that the groups that manage such conversations are self-regulating. At a recent Cannes Lion seminar, 'Can Brands Be Friends?'[21] Blake Chandlee from Facebook and Jay Stevens from MySpace, commented on how brands actually get support from their communities when those brands are criticised.

In the face of this, we are seeing the rise of a new discipline: social media marketing (SMM), the monitoring and promotion of brands within social media sites. The beginnings of this are evident through the facility on Facebook and LinkedIn to create company groups and webpages and with through the creation of applications that allow users to track the blogsphere, such as Google's Hot Trends[22] and Nielsen's Buzz Metrics.[23] But SMM is much more than this. It involves actively engaging with communities by posting comments, answering questions and adding value within online communities – the sort of communications you might naturally have with colleagues in the course of a day at work.

Substantial amounts of research are highlighting the importance of relationships with colleagues at work, and, although this in itself is nothing new, its significance the assessment of the deal on offer has grown. It is therefore no surprise that people believe more about what an organisation has to offer or is doing when they hear it from friends and colleagues than when they read it on a website or hear about it from management.

Employer brands must address this new development – and there are some obvious routes which surprisingly few organisations are taking advantage of. Alumni management is one of them. In this hyper-connected world, where the average Generation Y candidate only expects to stay in the same job for two years or less, the power of alumni networks is something that organisations will need to capitalise on.

The professional services firms are probably the best at this, accepting that they are likely to lose a percentage of people and knowing that when an accountant leaves, they are more than likely to turn into a client opportunity somewhere else.

The expression 'boomerang hiring' has been used by organisations like Enterprise Rent-A-Car, which actively pursues this strategy. Not only does it mean that leavers are more likely to be brand ambassadors, but their brand advocacy is

---

21   http://www.canneslions.com/festival/seminar_detail.cfm?workshop_id=50.
22   http://www.google.com/trends.
23   http://www.nielsenbuzzmetrics.com.

strengthened by returning to their original firm and the business gains massive cost advantages by re-recruiting proven talent. As Donna Miller, European HR Director of Enterprise Rent-A-Car says, 'The returning employee is every bit as big a compliment to your brand and HR strategy as the retained employee, and they may have picked up extra training and skills in their time away.'[24]

Networking technology – like that used by Facebook and LinkedIn – is an obvious route to use in alumni management, and companies like IBM are looking into social network analysis systems that enable them to capitalise on their employees' networks. IBM Connection[25] and The Greater IBM connection[26] are two such examples. From a company perspective, the organisation gains access to a broad talent pool at a fraction of the cost; from a candidate perspective, they gain access to research, industry leaders, useful tools and applications that might otherwise be beyond their reach. As IBM puts it, 'There's no cost to be a Greater IBMer – ever. What's not to like?'

Of course there is one aspect of 'belonging' that organisations have successfully explored – employee referrals for recruitment. Again, this has been boosted by technology in recent years, although, at the same time, some aspects of diversity are potentially challenged by those referring 'in their mould'. By this we mean that those individuals who refer potential employees can do so because they are 'like themselves' and therefore any stereotypes that might exist are sustained.

Employer brands of the future will recognise that our need to belong differs from what it was in the past – loyalty has been redefined. The deal needs to feel more intrinsic and more individual.

The Best Employer Brands in the Next Decade will be Leader Brands

As we entered the twenty-first century our Omnicom sister company, Interbrand, published a book featuring 25 views on the future of brands.[27] The authors' conclusions, which also drew on studies of 2,500 brands worldwide, on what would lie behind the most successful brands going forward is compelling

---

24 'Attract Boomerang Hires', Personneltoday.com, 1 October 2007.
25 https://www.ibmconnection.com.
26 http://www.ibm.com/ibm/greateribm.
27 Rita Clifton and Esther Maghan, *The Future of Brands*, Macmillan Business, Basingstoke, 2000.

reading, and I make no apologies for taking their three themes and applying them to employer branding.

Clarity and *consistency* lay behind the most successful brands to date – and there is much in both the theoretical argument and the case studies contained within this book that resonates for employer brands. However, the authors suggest that these will merely be hygiene factors for brands in the future. Far more important will be *leadership*, by which they mean a brand 'that leads people through an overloaded and complex future, and that leads standards – not just at the level of product, service and creative quality but increasingly at the level of values and proactive social contribution'.

It is easy to relate this to the world of the employer – reinforcing so much of what we have covered in our book and emphasised in this closing chapter. The employer brands that will win in the future are those that manage their employer reputation holistically and inside out. This is not about reputation management in the 'spin doctor' way we have come to associate with so much of today's world. Rather this is about reputation management being integral to organisational performance and success. You might even dare to call it strategic cultural management – but, then, that is another book.

Index

4-C recruitment marketing
    framework 86–8
advertising 115–20, 203
AIDS 68
alumni management 209–10
Amazon 201
attendance awards 131–2
Audit Commission 134–5

BAPB (Bold, Authentic,
    Pragmatic and Breaking
    the Mould) 112–13
benchmarking 83, 186–7
blogs 203, 207
BMW 21
Body Shop 7
boomerang hiring 209–10
Bradford Management School 4–5
brand alignment 30
brand balance model 42–3, 180
brand management 4–6
brand research 60–61
brand rituals 84
brand transparency 14–15
brand values 94
Branded Houses 49
Branding HR 133–4
brands 6–8
    performance of 80
business cases 188–91
buying 95

candidate research 76
causality 187
CBS (Competition Beating
    Service) 143–4
CEOs 164
charities 46, 199
CIP (University of Cambridge
    Programme for Industry) 198
circles of love 84
co-branding 199
coaches 97
communication 111, 144
Competition Beating Service
    (CBS) 143–4
conflict 113–14
consumer impact 175
consumer research 50–51
corporate social responsibility
    (CSR) 194–9
culture 64–7, 110, 139–40
customer experience 83
customer service 95–6, 125, 141

digital world 199–201, 203
diversity 75

emotional commitment 37–8
employee experience 23–4
employee insights 86
employee value proposition
    (EVP) 20–23

development 30–31
global 76–80
validation 31
employees *see also* employee
    value proposition (EVP)
benefits 132–3, 198
celebrations 132
as consumers 5
engagement *see* engagement
feedback 100
high-maintenance
    behaviours 13–14
loyalty 8, 13–14
performance 97, 126, 136
retention 141–2, 172
suggestion schemes 130
touchpoints 51–6
well-being 198–9
employer brand managers 164–5
employer brand strength 171–2
employer branding
    definition 17–20, 61–2
    global 57–70, 207–8
    importance of 105
    methodology 25–33
    origins 3–6
    ownership 151–65
    process monitoring 177–8
    purpose of 62–4
    segmentation 21–3
employers of choice 25
endorsed Branded Houses 49
engagement
    business success 144–5
    communications 133
    definition 36–9
    discretionary effort 9
    impact 174–5
    metrics 168
    programmes and policies 129–33

psychological contracts 41
surveys 86
travel industry 55–6
Enterprise Rent-A-Car 153–4, 209–10
EVP *see* employee value proposition

Facebook 207, 208–9
financial impact 175
Financial Times Top 50 Best
    Workplaces 134
focus groups 107
4-C recruitment marketing
    framework 86–8

Generation Y 13–14, 207
GlaxoSmithKline 21, 103–20, 159–60
global employee value
    propositions 76–80
global employer branding
    57–70, 207–8
glocalisation 208
Godber, Mary 125
graduate research 83

HBOS 47, 203
Hertfordshire Constabulary 187
House of Brands model 47–8
HR *see* human resources
HSBC 198
human capital management 171–2
human capital metrics 168
human resources 99, 139–40
    metrics 168
    newsletters 132

IBM 210
ideological contracts 41
IIP (Investors in People) 128–9
impact 169–75
implementation of employer

brand 31–2
intangible assets 12
intellectual capital 12
internship programmes 85
Investors in People 128–9

Jamie's School Dinners 39
job satisfaction 127–8

Knowledge Lab 201

language 61
leadership 44, 172, 211
London & Quadrant Housing
        Trust 121–36
long service awards 130
love 86–8
luggage-handling systems 68
LVMH group 47

management training 126–7
Marconi 60
marketing of recruitment 82
Marks & Spencer 89–101, 199
M&As (mergers and acquisitions)
        43–6, 135–6
MBTI (Myers-Briggs Type
        Indicator) 68
measurement of success 32–3,
        166–9 *see also* metrics
mergers and acquisitions
        (M&As) 43–6, 135–6
metrics
    cost of 183
    cycle of 169–71
    engagement 168
    human capital 168
    human resources 168
    impact 171–5
    process 178–82

selection of 183–4
timing of 187–8
usefulness of 184–6
Ministry of Justice 157–8
motivation 128–9
Myers-Briggs Type Indicator
        (MBTI) 68

NCR 201
Nike 201

Orange 38, 60, 69

parent culture 64–7
paternalism 8
pay 96–7
performance of employees
        97, 126, 136
Philips 73–88
process metrics 178–82
professional qualifications
        132
psychological contracts
        8–11, 39–42, 67

rational commitment 38
recruitment
    advertising 78–9, 115–20
    communications 4, 84–5
    impact 174
    marketing of 82
    referrals 210
    screening 142
relational contracts 40–41
reputation 44–5, 164, 172
research 28–9, 60–61
return on investment 176–7
rewards 96, 198
risk and reward 67
Rose, Stuart 94

Royal Bank of Scotland 47,
    161–3, 171–2, 189–91
Royal Mail 155–6

satisfaction surveys 86, 126
school dinners 39
sickness absence 131–2, 172, 198
social media marketing (SMM) 209
social network analysis systems 210
social networks 201, 207, 208–9
staff *see* employees
Starbucks 84
The Sunday Times 100 Best Companies
    To Work For 134

talent war 11–12, 82
Tesco 22–3
touchpoints
    behavioural content 54–6
    candidates 74
    consistency through 77–8
    consumers 50–51
    dimensions 53–6
    employees 51–6
    look and feel 53

tone of voice 53–4
training 96, 97, 126–7
transactional contracts 40
travel industry 46–7, 55–6

unique selling propositions (USP) 6
University of Cambridge Programme
    for Industry (CIP) 198
US Army Online Recruitment
    Game 203
USP (unique selling propositions) 6

value profit chains 44
Virgin Group 49
Virgin Mobile 38
virtuous circle 97–9
visioning 27–8

Wall Street Journal Careers Fair 203
war for talent 11–12, 82
Web 2.0 200–201
websites 200–201
William Hill plc 137–47

Yell 201

If you have found this resource useful you may be interested in other titles from Gower

MBA Management Models
Sue Harding and Trevor Long
Paperback: 240 pages: 978-0-566-08137-8

The CEO: Chief Engagement Officer
Turning Hierarchy Upside Down to Drive Performance
John Smythe
Paperback: 226 pages: 978-0-566-08561-1

Making the Connections:
Using Internal Communication to Turn Strategy into Action
Bill Quirke
Paperback: 384 pages: 978-0-566-08780-6

Grass Roots Leaders:
The BrainSmart Revolution in Business
Tony Buzan, Tony Dottino and Richard Israel
Hardback: 258 pages: 978-0-566-08802-5

Communicating Strategy
Phil Jones
Paperback: 198 pages: 978-0-566-08810-0

GOWER